Crossroads and Connections

CWU Art Alumni Exhibition

Crossroads and Connections

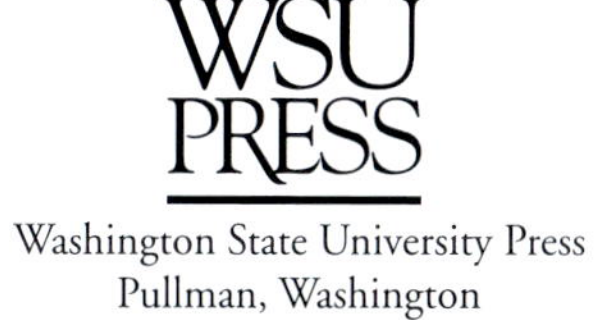

Washington State University Press
Pullman, Washington

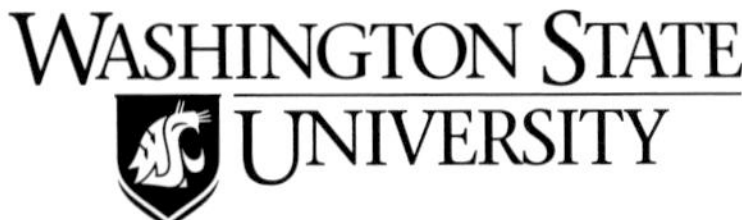

Washington State University Press
PO Box 645910
Pullman, Washington 99164-5910
Phone: 800-354-7360
Fax: 509-335-8568
E-mail: wsupress@wsu.edu
Web Site: wsupress.wsu.edu

First printing 2008

Library of Congress Cataloging-in-Publication Data

Central Washington University art alumni exhibition : crossroads and connections.
p. cm.
Includes index.
ISBN 978-0-87422-300-2 (alk. paper)
1. Art, American--20th century--Exhibitions. 2. Art, American--21st century--Exhibitions. 3. Central Washington University--Alumni and alumnae--Exhibitions. I. Central Washington University.
N6512.C415 2008
709.797'07479757--dc22

On the Cover: Nancy Worden's *Exosquellette #2*, 2003, from the *Exosquellette* series.

The necklace, made of silver, copper, bone, wood, glass, and nickel, is intended to protect the wearer from a variety of different emotional and spiritual situations, and is a potent commentary on women's roles in society.

French for exoskeleton, *Exosquellette #2* was created from clothespins. Worden's artwork is known for its societal statements and the materials used—primarily found objects such as keys, coins, eyeglass lenses, and fresh roses.

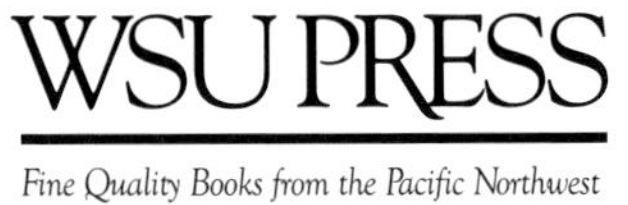

Acknowledgements

First and foremost, I would like to thank the alumni artists who participated in the *CWU Art Alumni Exhibition: Crossroads and Connections*. Not only did their dedication and creativity make the 2007 exhibition possible, it was the suggestions of alumni that provided the impetus for both the exhibition and accompanying catalog.

Dean of the College of Arts and Humanities, Marji Morgan, supplied the vision for this endeavor, as well as the necessary resources and contacts to see it through to its fruition. College of Arts and Humanities Development Officer, Catherine Scarlett, is to be commended for compiling the alumni records and corresponding with numerous alumni artists. Emeritus faculty who put together valuable contact lists of their former students included John Agars, Cynthia Krieble, Louis Kollmeyer, Chris Papadopoulos, and Constance Speth. It is through the commitment of such faculty that the Department of Art has left a strong legacy of active artists and arts educators.

I would also like to thank past and present Gallery One Visual Arts Center staff members, including Kent Swanson, Heidi Sherwin, Mauri Johnson, and Renee Adams, for their collaborative spirit and support during the exhibition.

I am especially grateful for the generous funding awarded by President Jerilyn S. McIntyre and the Office of the President, without which this catalog would not have been published. Bruce Porter, director of Business Services and Contracts, and Becky Watson, director of Public Relations and Marketing, are to be thanked for their efforts in securing the catalog's funding, contract, and for donating countless staff hours toward its completion. Public Relations and Marketing Writer Liz Bryson composed the artists' profiles, edited the copy, and was indispensable in coordinating the catalog's publication. Thanks are also extended to the department's Photographer, Richard Villacres, for his impeccable photography, and to Designers Rosario Herrera, Bret Bleggi, and Becky Watson for their striking design.

Lastly, I would like to acknowledge our exhibition sponsors, the CWU Foundation's Carrico Endowment, and express gratitude for the ongoing funding provided by the Associated Students of Central Washington University, and the Catherine Nisbet Memorial Endowment. It is their commitment to the arts at Central Washington University that makes the exhibitions at Sarah Spurgeon Gallery possible.

Heather Horn Johnson
Manager, Sarah Spurgeon Gallery

Introduction

The Central Washington University Department of Art has been producing outstanding graduates for decades. Many of these graduates are practicing artists in all areas of artistic endeavor. Although their memories of student days at Central are vivid, most CWU artist alumni had not exhibited their work on campus until 2007. In April 2007, fifty-eight Central art graduates from all over the country presented their work in the *CWU Art Alumni Exhibition: Crossroads and Connections*. The exhibition and this catalog are a celebration of their creativity, passion, and success.

Crossroads and Connections very appropriately sums up the themes underlying the exhibition. In thinking about what happens to students after they graduate and become alumni, the word crossroads comes to mind. Every artist represented here has faced many of them, including the question of whether or not to continue creating art. Furthermore, the exhibition stressed the connections, or re-connections, between art alumni who had not seen each other in years, between art alums and faculty, and alums and the Central campus. The exhibition also connected former art students to future ones through the new Art Alumni Scholarship launched at the exhibition opening. Finally, *Crossroads and Connections* brought our university and town together, as artists' work was displayed at both the CWU Sarah Spurgeon Gallery and the Gallery One Visual Arts Center in downtown Ellensburg, Washington.

Crossroad and Connections featured the work of alumni artists who received their Central degree prior to 1980. Each artist had two pieces displayed in the exhibition, one of which is pictured in this catalog. An illustration of each individual's work is accompanied by a brief biography and a quote about their artistic endeavors. Although many genres, styles, and philosophies are represented here, they all share the excellence and originality for which CWU's Department of Art is known. With this catalog, we thank the many Department of Art faculty members, past and present, whose dedication and outstanding teaching have inspired these and so many other CWU art students over the years.

Marji Morgan, Dean
College of Arts and Humanities

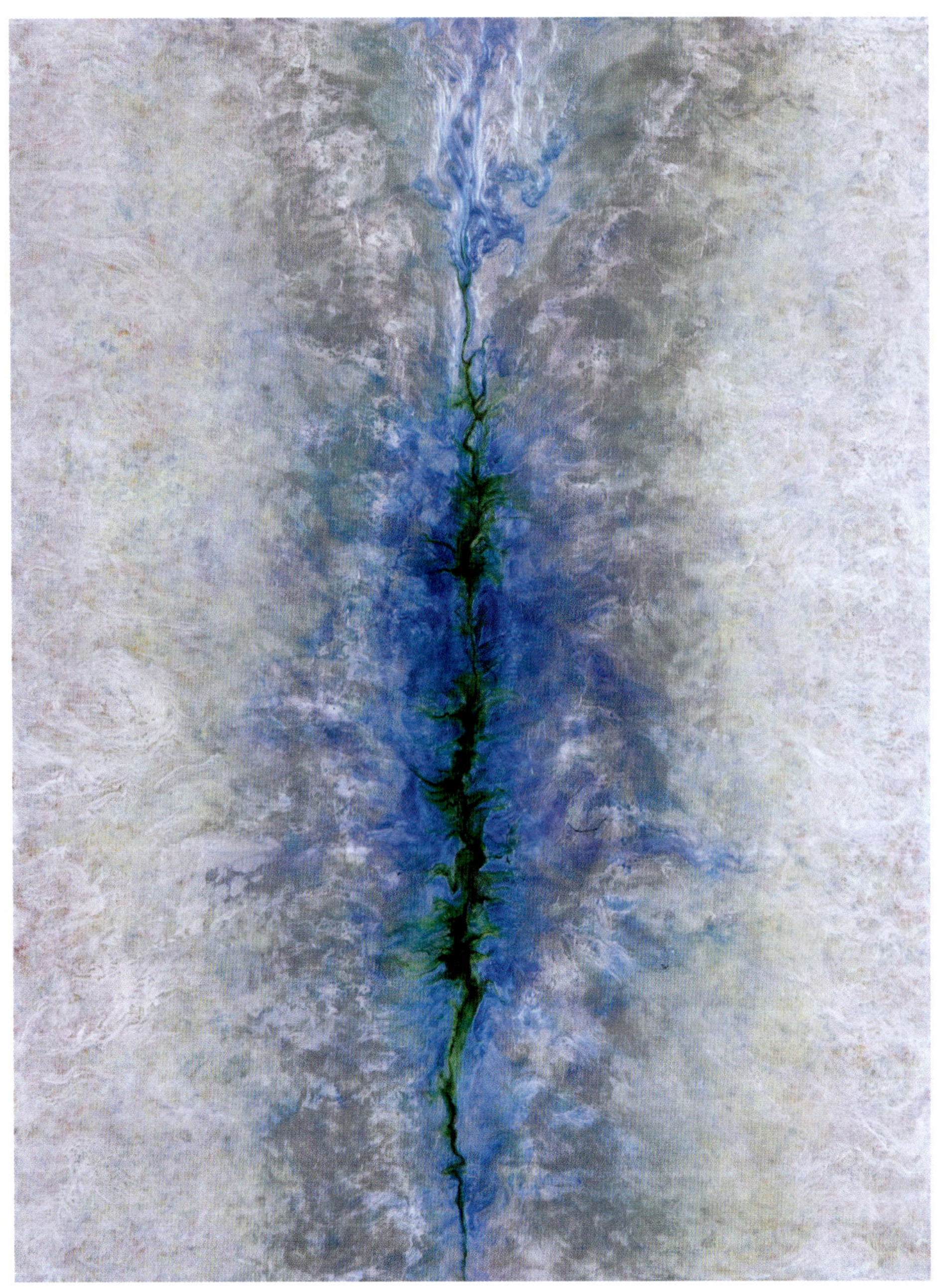

Euphoric Sky, 2006, acrylic on canvas, 31¾ x 41½ in.

Sam Albright

Class of 1978

Ellensburg, Washington sculptor and painter Sam Albright finds it challenging as an artist to combine unrelated elements into one. It is a method he used not only with his art, but also throughout his personal life.

Albright, who graduated with an emphasis in painting and sculpture, cites his home as a good example. Albright resides on forty acres with his wife, Ren, several goats, chickens, horses, and other animals. He is presently working to combine a sustainable agricultural environment along with his art; an area he calls an "art farm." While painting, Albright explores "transitional zones, inspired by the natural world and the interior world of mind, psychology, and consciousness."

Albright has exhibited his paintings, sculptures, and jewelry in several solo and juried exhibitions throughout the Pacific Northwest, including Allied Arts of Yakima Valley, Yakima, Washington, the Henry Art Gallery, and the Center on Contemporary Art, both in Seattle, Washington. He took several years off from art to pursue other interests, but is now back in the studio full time.

Recent Career Highlights

- 2006: Inner Eye series of acrylic paintings at Brazillis Gallery, Seattle, Washington
- 2005: Oil painting featured in Allied Arts of Yakima Valley juried exhibition, Yakima, Washington
- 2005: Custom furniture commission, Tara Mandala Retreat Center, Pagosa Springs, Colorado

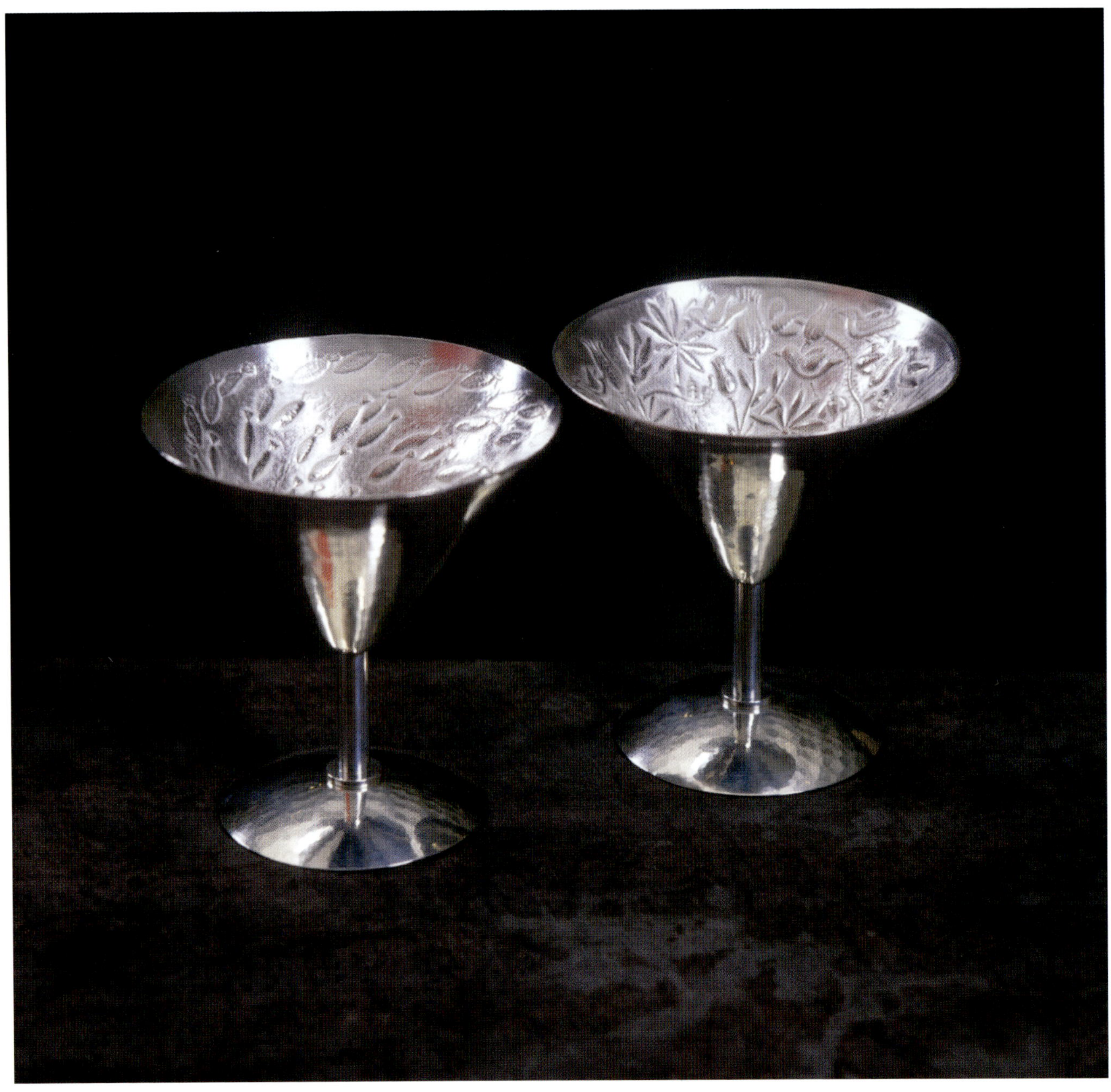

What's at the Bottom of the Well?, 2007, sterling and fine silver, 4¾ x 4¾ in.

Candace Beardslee

Class of 1974

Candace Beardslee, an art education graduate, has spent most of her life entangled in a love affair with metalwork.

"The idea that I can change a flat sheet of metal into a vessel by using a hammer and a t-stake amazes me," she said. "I still marvel that something as rigid as a piece of metal can be so malleable."

Beardslee, a Duvall, Washington resident, spends most of her time working as a self-employed artist, and focuses on hollowware and jewelry. She recently participated in the 2006 Artist Trust Exhibition at the Chase Gallery in Spokane, Washington. She has also shown artwork at Washington State's Bellevue Art Museum, the Tacoma Art Museum, and the Seattle Art Museum, as well as the Society of Arts and Crafts in Boston, Massachusetts.

Colleagues have appreciated her work over the decades and presented her with several awards, including the Pacific Northwest Annual Juror's Award at the Bellevue Art Museum in Bellevue, Washington.

Career Highlights

- Current work in the collection of the Victoria and Albert Museum, London, England
- 2001 and 2006: Artist Trust Gap Grant, Seattle, Washington
- 2005: Looking Forward, Glancing Back: Northwest Designer Craftsmen at 50, Bellevue Art Museum, Bellevue, Washington

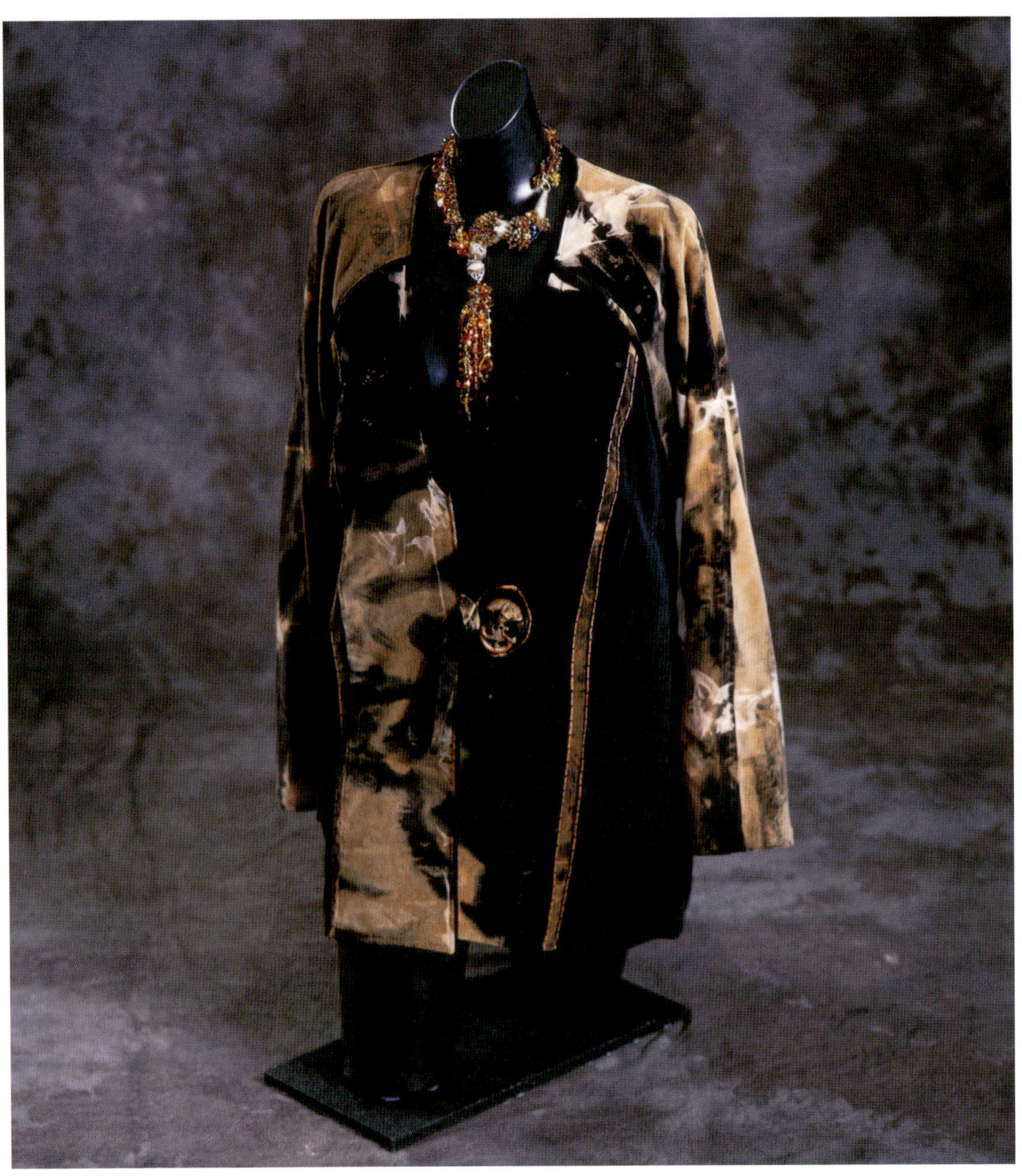

Necklace: *Terra Incognita, Coral Snake*, 2002, sterling silver, stones, and beads, 17¾ x ¾ in.
Jacket: *Grand Canal*, 2006, discharged cotton velveteen, 61 x 31½ x 1 in.

Ann Marta Bowker

Class of 1957

Ann Marta Bowker, a Moxee, Washington resident, started her art career as a child, experimenting with many forms. As a professional, she focuses on textiles and jewelry, and has also written and produced plays for children, as well as choreographed musicals.

"My favorite kind of work is whatever I'm doing, and my best piece is the next one," she said. "The process of creating has been central to my life since I was a child. Now I am working primarily with fabric and jewelry, although I still dip back into painting, my primary expression for many years."

Bowker has exhibited her work at several galleries, including the Allied Arts of Yakima Valley, Yakima, Washington, the Clymer Museum of Art in Ellensburg, Washington, and the International Quilt Festival in Houston, Texas. She works with private collectors throughout the United States and Canada, including one who has purchased more than 150 pieces of her wearable art and jewelry.

Recent Career Highlights

- 2006: Juried exhibition, Allied Arts of Yakima Valley, Yakima, Washington
- 2005: (And multiple years prior) Fairfield/Bernina Fashion Show participant, Houston, Texas
- 2004: Arts Woman of the Year, Larson Gallery Guild, Yakima, Washington

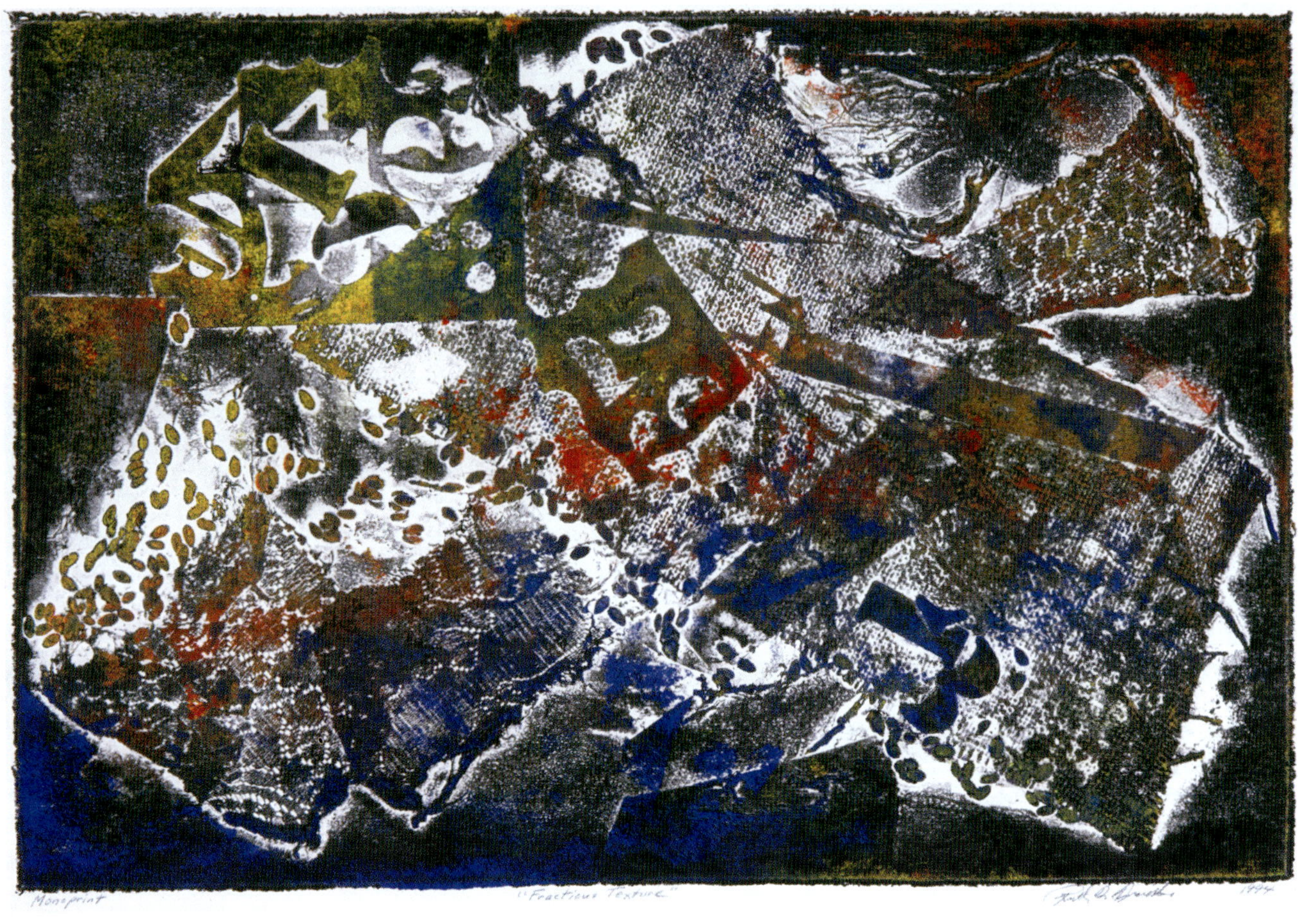

Fractious Texture, 1994, monoprint, 23⅜ x 16 in.

Ruth F. Bravetti

Class of 1970 and 1972

Ruth F. Bravetti, an Olympia, Washington resident, graduated from Central Washington University with a bachelor of arts degree in 1970 and a master of arts in 1972. She has spent most of her life teaching art and math, while personally focusing on printmaking.

"I have completed some drawings and paintings in the last few years, but most of my recent work has involved creating mixed media printmaking images. Printmaking, with its endless textures and techniques, is still my main area of interest," Bravetti said.

Bravetti builds plates for printing and uses a variety of materials, such as plexiglass, wood, linoleum, and cardboard. Her students often inspire her work.

"A great deal of my current studio work is influenced by my high school students. They are an endless source of ideas for present and future images," Bravetti said. "I have also created some of my work, especially pottery, as demonstrations for my students."

Recent Career Highlights

- 2004-2006: Print Zero Studios Print Exchange participant, Seattle, Washington
- 2002: Developed a visual fine arts program for the Oakville School District, Oakville, Washington
- 1994-1995: Co-authored Kent School District's curricula for art and math, Kent, Washington

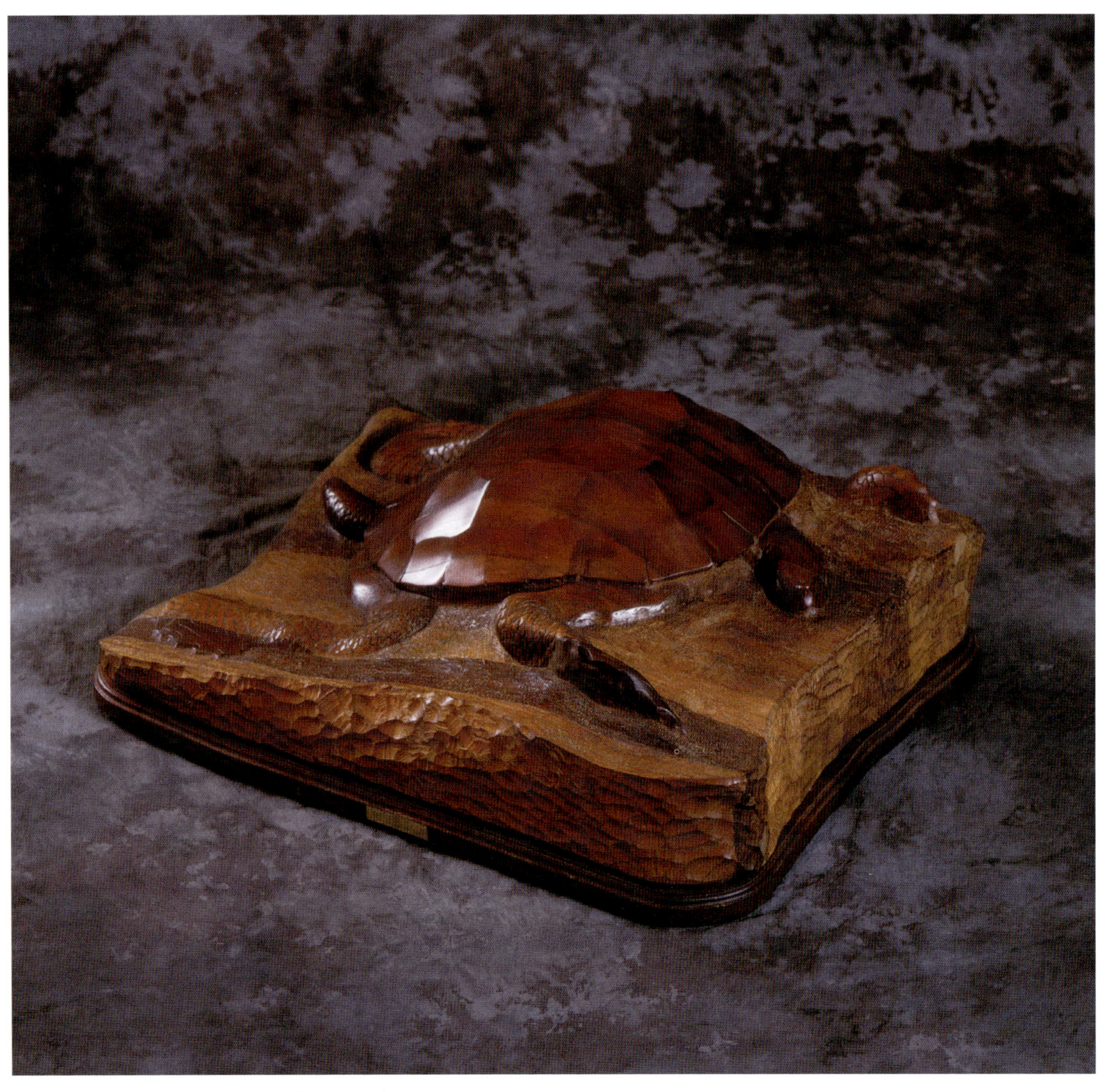

Myrtle the Turtle, 1994, Honduras mahogany, 35 x 25 x 12 in.

Carl W. Brodin

Class of 1964 and 1968

Born in Minneapolis, Minnesota, Carl W. Brodin lived in several states before coming to Washington State, where he graduated from Central Washington University with both a bachelor's and master's degree in art education.

Brodin, who passed away in January of 2008, was active in many art communities across Washington, including Chehalis and Centralia.

"I was instrumental in [the] formation of the Southwest Washington Art League, and served as its first, second, and fourth president before leaving Chehalis, Washington," he said. "I also taught art at Clover Park High School, and adult education at Pierce College and McNeil Island Corrections Center in Pierce County, Washington, until retirement."

Brodin worked extensively in several mediums, including sculpture. Some of his preferred sculpture materials included mahogany, white oak, black walnut, sandstone, marble, and metal. He also created oil and watercolor paintings, as well as charcoal and chalk images.

Recent Career Highlights

- Work installed in the U.S. Navy SeaBee Museum's permanent collection, Gulfport, Mississippi
- Clover Park High School art teacher
- Received a "first expert" blue ribbon in the Northwest Carvers show for *Myrtle the Turtle*

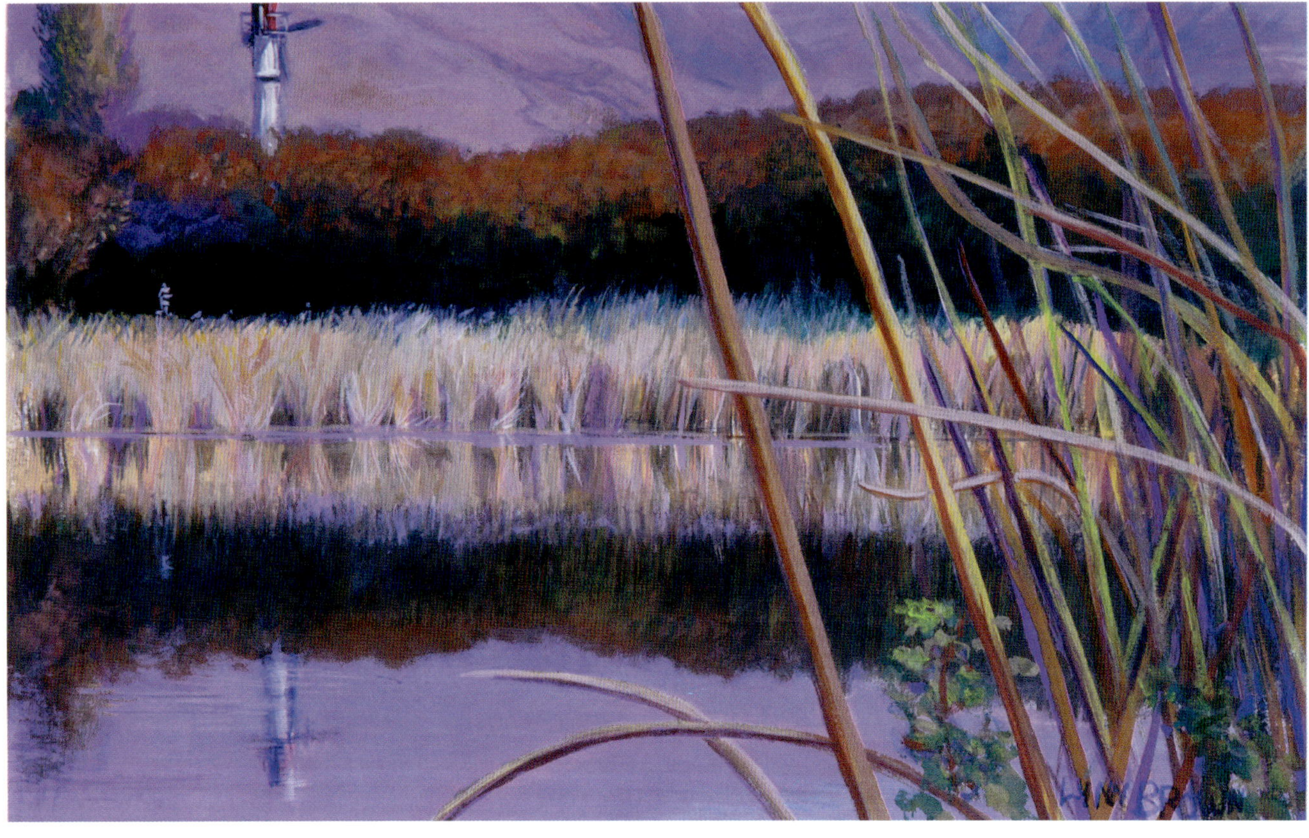

Reed Reflections, 2007, acrylic, 22¼ x 13½ in.

Lynn Wright Brown

Class of 1978

For the past several years, Lynn Wright Brown has focused her artistic talents on pastel and acrylic paintings, primarily of local landscapes. The Wenatchee, Washington resident said she finds pastels especially challenging "because of the many ways to layer and blend colors."

Brown graduated from Central Washington University with a master's degree in education.

"More recently I have been doing children and animal portraits. In the past I have worked in printmaking, mostly serigraphs and monotypes. I have been challenged to try to achieve that kind of luminosity with the two very different medias of acrylics and pastels."

Prior to attending CWU, Brown worked as a graphic artist in Minneapolis, Minnesota, and Chicago, Illinois. During her time as a designer, she created an emergency medical information symbol that is still used on emergency services vehicles, she said.

Recent Career Highlights

- Current works at Allisons of Manson Gallery, Manson, Washington
- 2006: Exhibit at Miller Gallery, Leavenworth, Washington
- 2000: Wenatchee Apple Blossom poster artist, Wenatchee, Washington

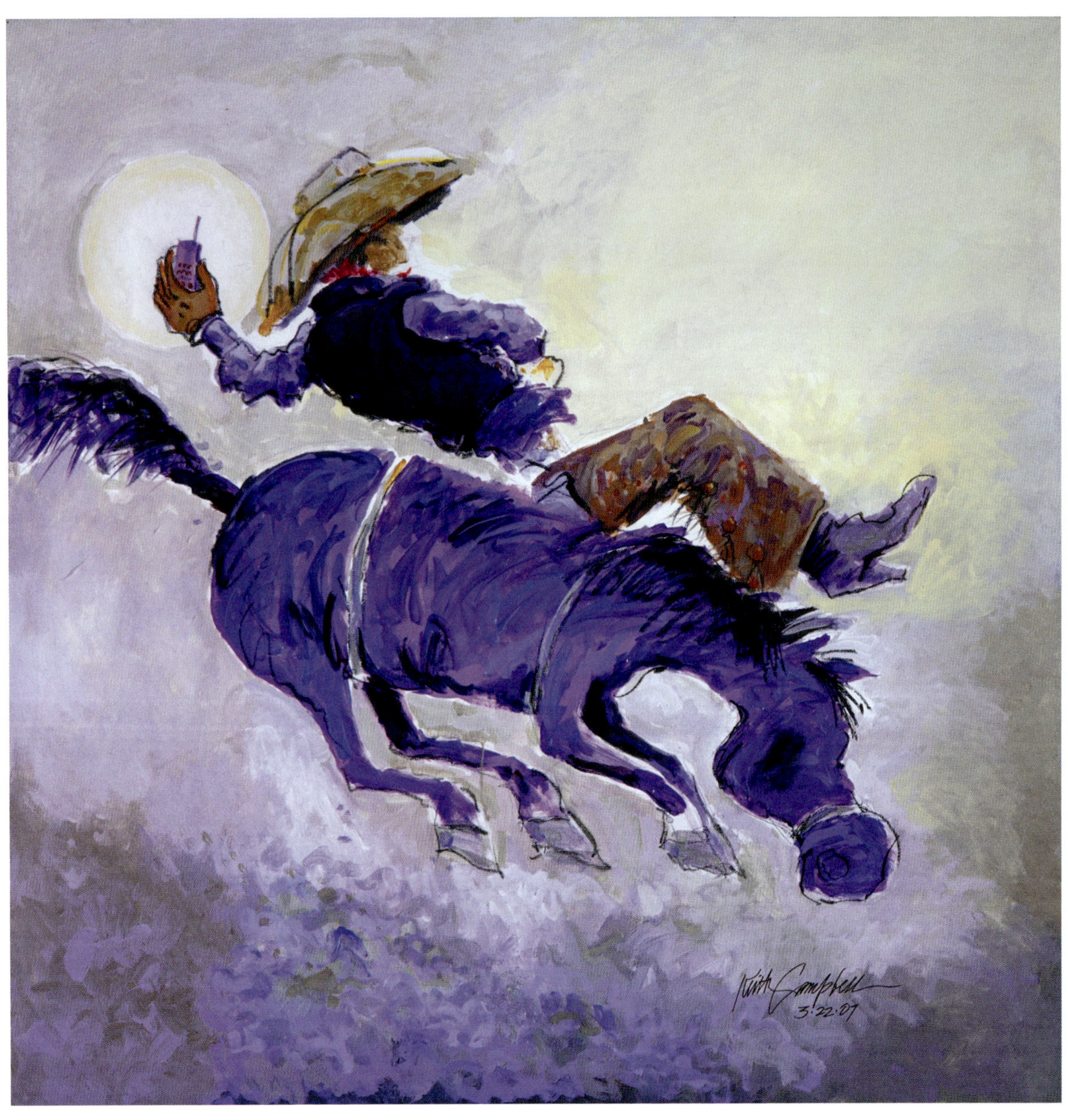

Can You Hear Me Now?, 2007, mixed media, 50 x 50 in.

Keith Campbell

Class of 1963

Before retiring in Gig Harbor, Washington, Keith Campbell spent forty years working as an advertising art director. During that time, he worked at several firms in Seattle, Washington and one in San Francisco, California.

"My expertise lies in bringing visual reality to a concept or idea, making it communicate simply, quickly, and strongly. I have an eye for typography and the color of a line of type. I also have an eye for lighting a product; not just technically, but emotionally for full impact," Campbell said.

Campbell graduated from Central Washington University with a bachelor of arts degree. In 1964 he graduated from the San Francisco Academy of Art in San Francisco, California.

Recent Career Highlights

- 2005: Northwest Addy and Clio gold awards for Parker Paint campaign, Seattle, Washington
- 1993-2005: Senior Art Director for Bonod & Remer Creative Marketing, Seattle, Washington
- 1967, 1986, and 1988: Winner of Best in Show from Seattle Art Directors, Seattle, Washington

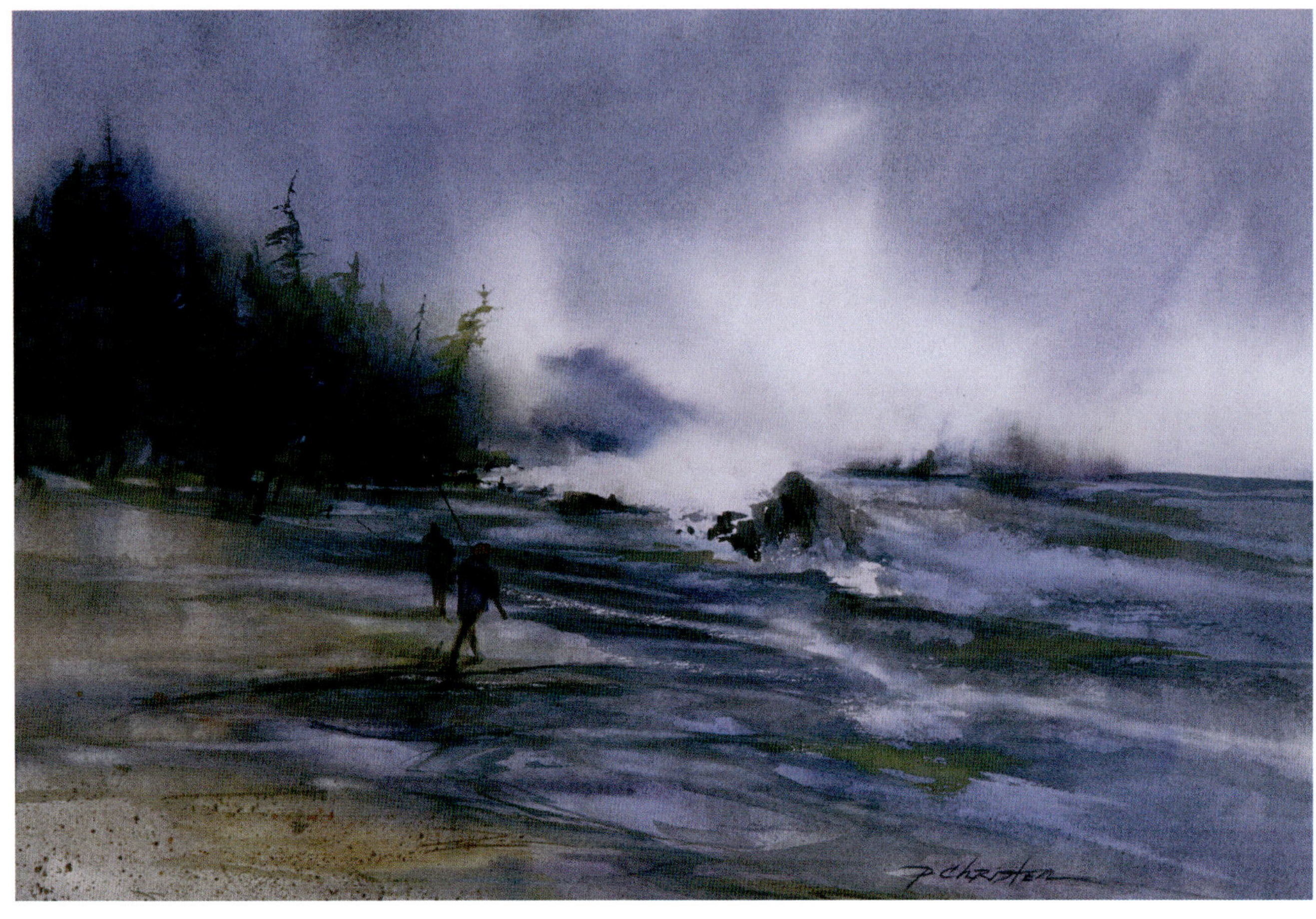

Carpe Diem, 2007, watercolor, 19½ x 12⅝ in.

Paula Christen

Class of 1976

Painter Paula Christen lives in Winthrop, Washington, where she exhibits her work in local and regional galleries. She focuses on watercolors and finds the surrounding landscapes of northern Washington inspiring.

"My paintings are predominately landscapes, containing elements of water, stone, and trees. I grew up in the Pacific Northwest and know these places best," she said. "These paintings are translations of the welcoming environment that I've experienced."

After graduating from Central Washington University in 1976 with a bachelor of arts degree, Christen became a member of the Northwest Watercolor Society of Bellevue, Washington, the Methow Arts Alliance in Twisp, Washington, and Winthrop Gallery, Winthrop, Washington. Her goal as a painter is "to be a strong link in the chain of artists whose works have inspired me."

"Each painting is a challenge to create, with bold form and juicy color, that is an improvement over the simple beauty of untouched white paper."

Recent Career Highlights

- 2007: Exhibit at the Lost River Winery, Winthrop, Washington
- 2006: Group exhibit at Winthrop Gallery, Winthrop, Washington
- 2005: Group exhibit at Depot Arts Center, Anacortes, Washington

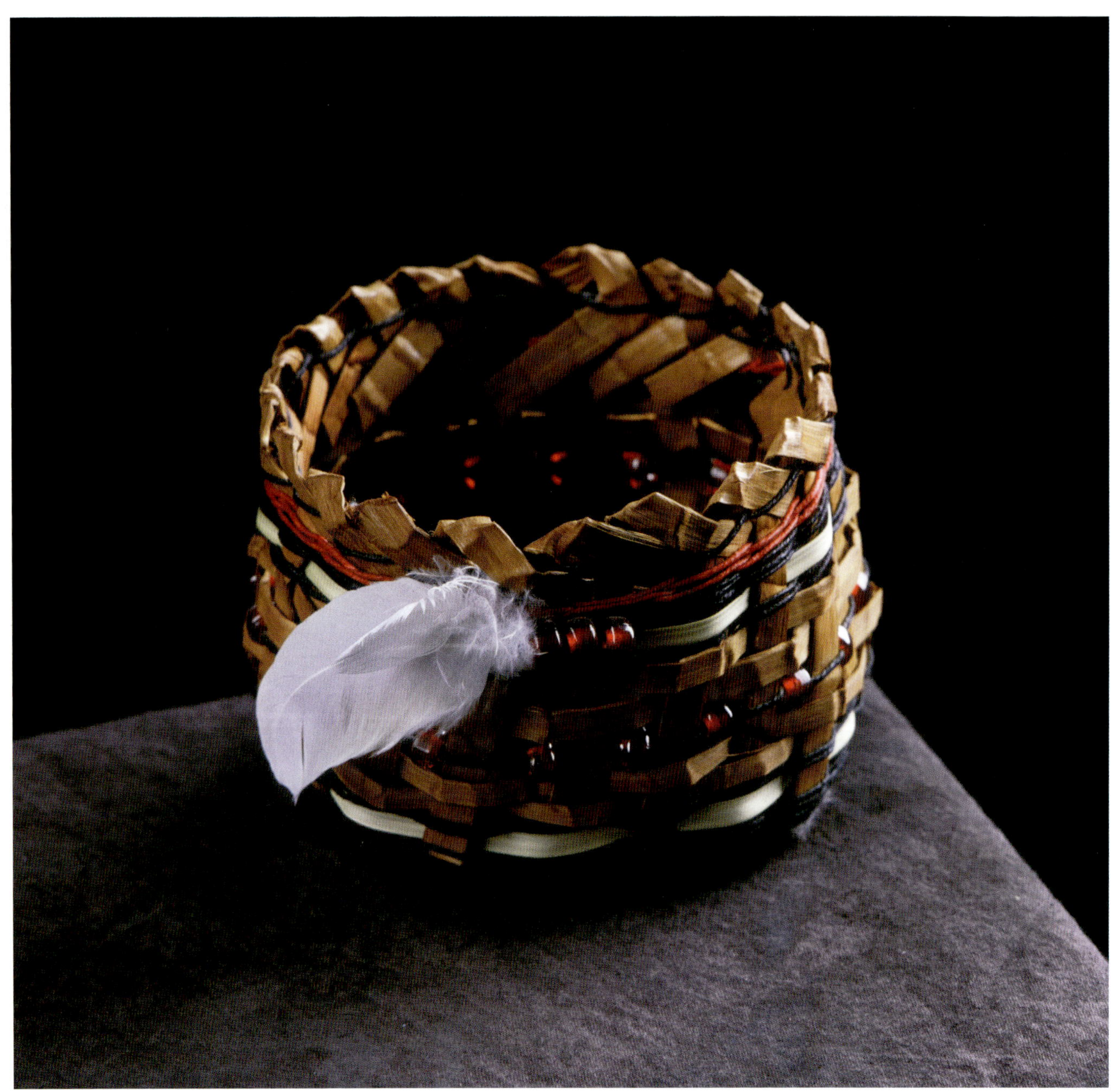

Pheasant Dreams, 2006, pine needles, waxed linen, mixed media, 4 x 4 x 2¼ in.

Laurie Cross

Class of 1976

Weaver Laurie Cross has been an artist-in-residence with Hood River, Oregon's Columbia Gorge Arts in Education program for seven years. During that time, Cross, a Husum, Washington resident, has taught basketry and worked on various art projects, including Mexican art in various schools.

"Since my acceptance into the Columbia Gorge Artists in Education program, I have focused for several years on teaching and learning new art forms to expand my teaching abilities," Cross said.

Her art is inspired by indigenous traditions and by her love of nature. She works with several weaving styles, techniques, and materials.

"Art for me is a synthesis of traditional and natural materials used to create an object of beauty and grace."

Since 1985, Cross has worked as the owner of The Hummingbird's Nest, located in Husum, where she teaches art. "Some of my adult classes include outings to gather and prepare natural materials. My adult students find my basketry classes boost their confidence in creativity."

Recent Career Highlights

- 2006: 27th Annual Artists of the Gorge Exhibition, Stevenson Community Library Gallery, Stevenson, Washington
- 2001: Co-coordinator of "Peace under Siege in Mexico," a photo exhibit at the Stevenson Community Library
- 1994: Instructor at the Native American Learning Center, Columbia Gorge Community College, The Dalles, Oregon

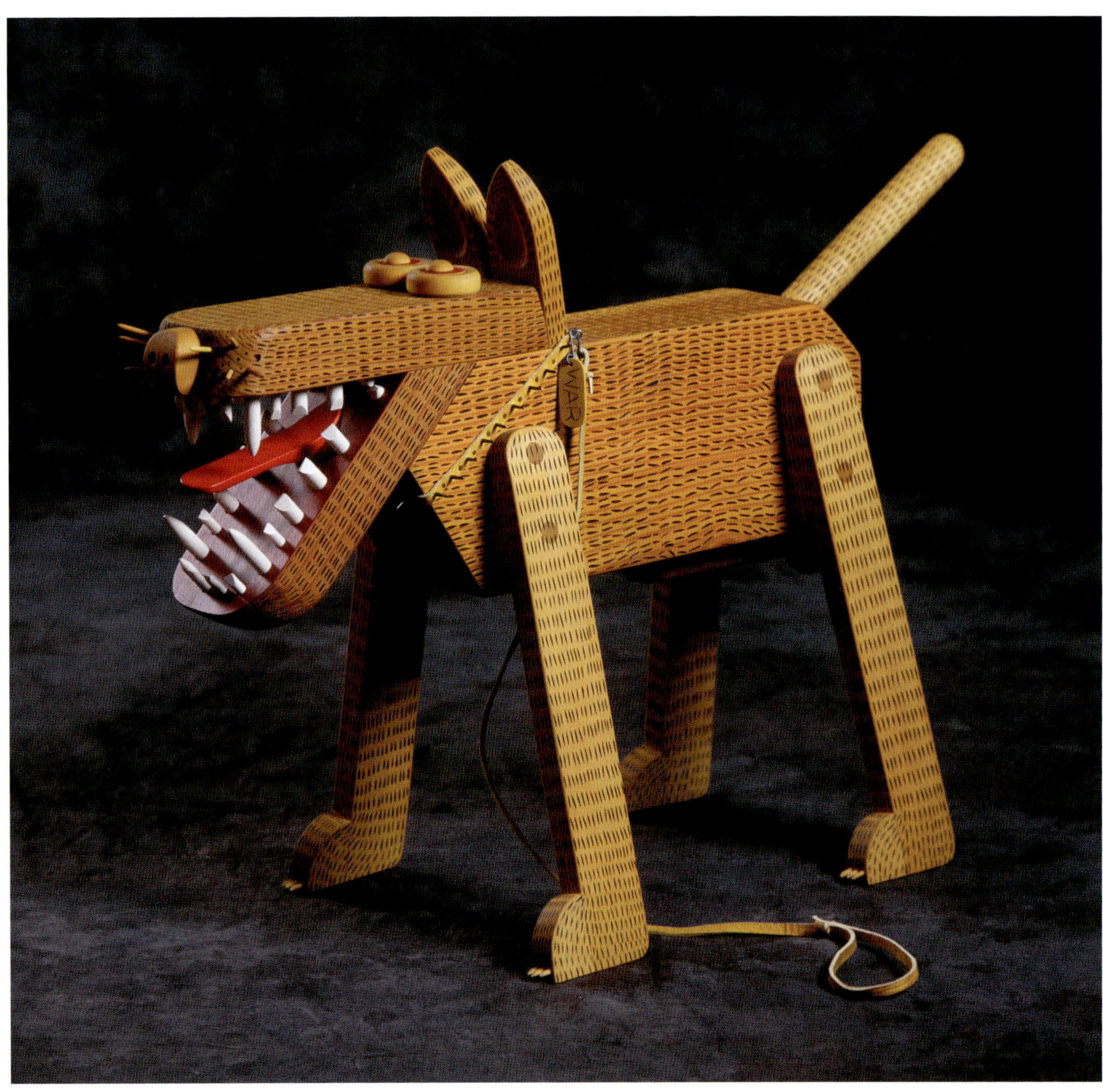

Dogs of War, 2003, mixed media, 26 x 9 x 18 in.

Darwin Davis

Class of 1957

Sculptor and illustrator Darwin Davis has a fascination with the plight of man.

"...Mr. Cro-Magnon could be considered the birth of creative dance and ever since, down through the ages, the visual and performing arts have played a major role in mankind's attempt to better understand the human condition. Hopefully, my work contributes something to that ongoing puzzlement," he said.

Davis graduated from Central Washington University in 1957 with a bachelor of arts degree. He is an Ellensburg, Washington native and has exhibited in many galleries in the area, as well as throughout the Pacific Northwest.

One of his recent exhibitions, at Ellensburg's Gallery One Visual Arts Center, was a retrospective of his work dating from the 1960s to 2006.

Davis also spent twenty-five years as a graphic designer for Central Washington University, from 1969 to 1994.

Recent Career Highlights

- 2006: Solo exhibit, Gallery One Visual Arts Center retrospective, Ellensburg, Washington
- 2006: Juried exhibit, Larson Gallery, Yakima, Washington
- 2006: Juried exhibit, Gallery One Visual Arts Center

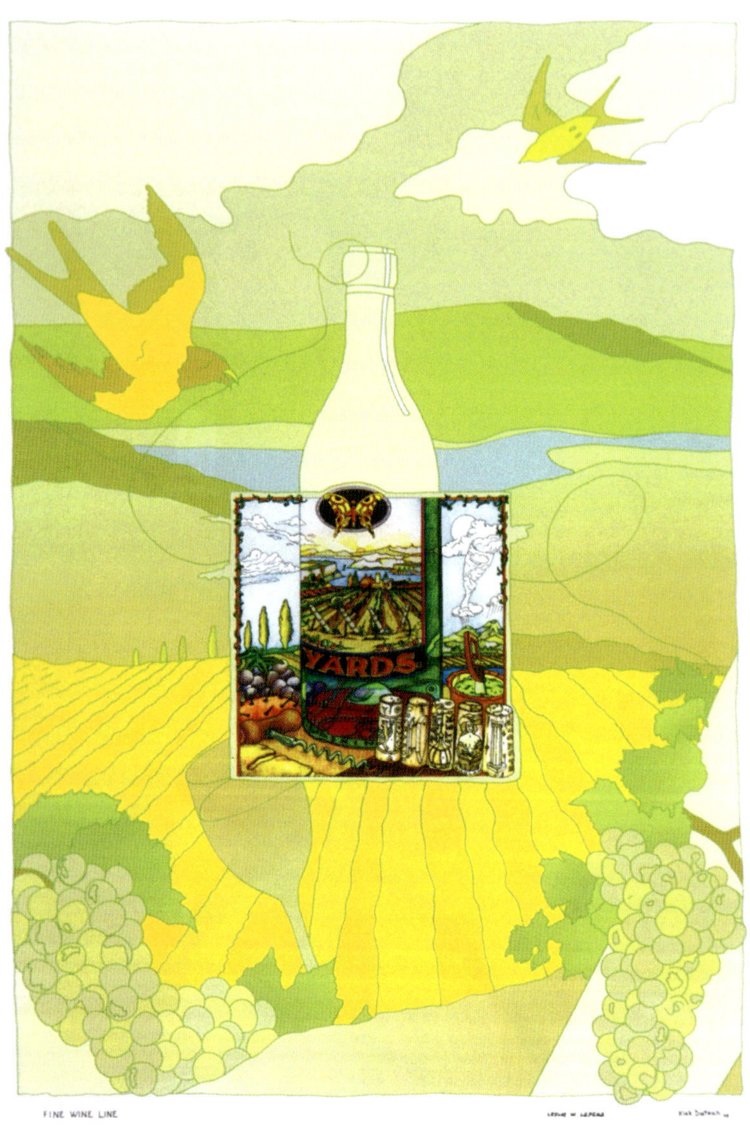

Fine Wine Line, 2005, giclée print, 19½ x 27½ in.

Kirk Dietrich

Class of 1975

East Wenatchee, Washington artist Kirk Dietrich graduated from Central Washington University with a bachelor of arts degree, and has since spent his professional career as a corporate identity artist and owner of the company Blind Renaissance, Inc., a creative, multi-media firm in East Wenatchee.

"I develop corporate identifications, logos, and packaging for companies, as well as original artwork and work in collaboration with other artists," Dietrich said.

He has owned his company since 1972, but has also worked as an art director for Excel Packaging Company in Cashmere, Washington, and as a graphic designer and illustrator for the Media Services Department at Wenatchee Valley College, Wenatchee, Washington.

Dietrich is also extremely active with local community service groups, and founded several organizations revolving around art education and performing arts.

Recent Career Highlights

- Robert Graves Gallery board member and past president, Wenatchee Valley College, Wenatchee, Washington
- Quest for Economic Development, original member and fundraising campaign developer, Wenatchee, Washington
- Founding member of Wenatchee's Performing Arts Center, Wenatchee, Washington

30

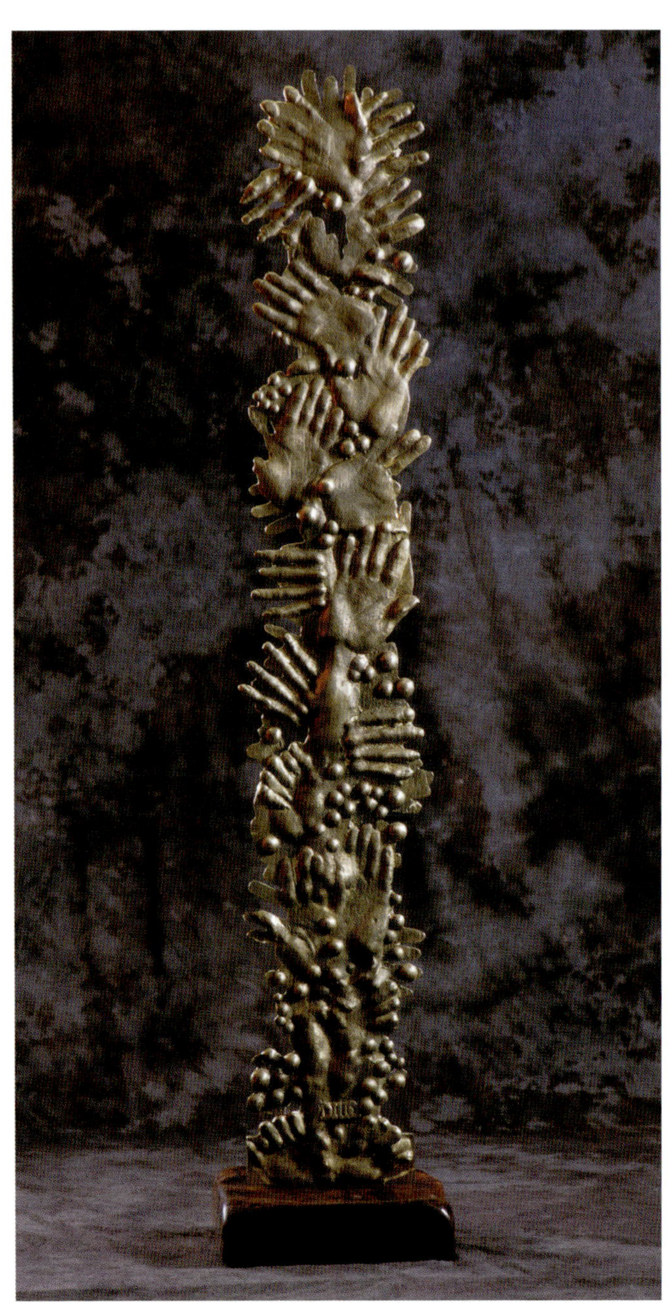

Hands, 2007, bronze, 13½ x 13½ x 68 in.

Bill Dilley
Class of 1971

Sculptor and painter Bill Dilley has spent most of his life on a twenty-five-acre Vashon Island, Washington ranch, where his peaceful surroundings have inspired his art.

"Drawing from my simplified life among the forests and fields, I have also mastered the art of painting, rock carving, and wood carving, for which I've won several awards," Dilley said. His earthy works are inspired by dreams, he once told a journalist.

He graduated from Central Washington University with a bachelor of arts degree and in 1973, graduated with a master of fine arts from the University of Washington.

Since then, he has exhibited in numerous venues across the Northwest, and also has work in many regional private collections. In 2003, he was featured in a *Sunset* magazine publication.

Recent Career Highlights

- 2006: Commission piece for Heathcrest Lane LLC, Westport, Washington
- 2004: Gallery 070 exhibition, Vashon Island, Washington
- 2000: People's Choice and Jurors's Choice award in the Mayor's Art Show, Eugene, Oregon

32

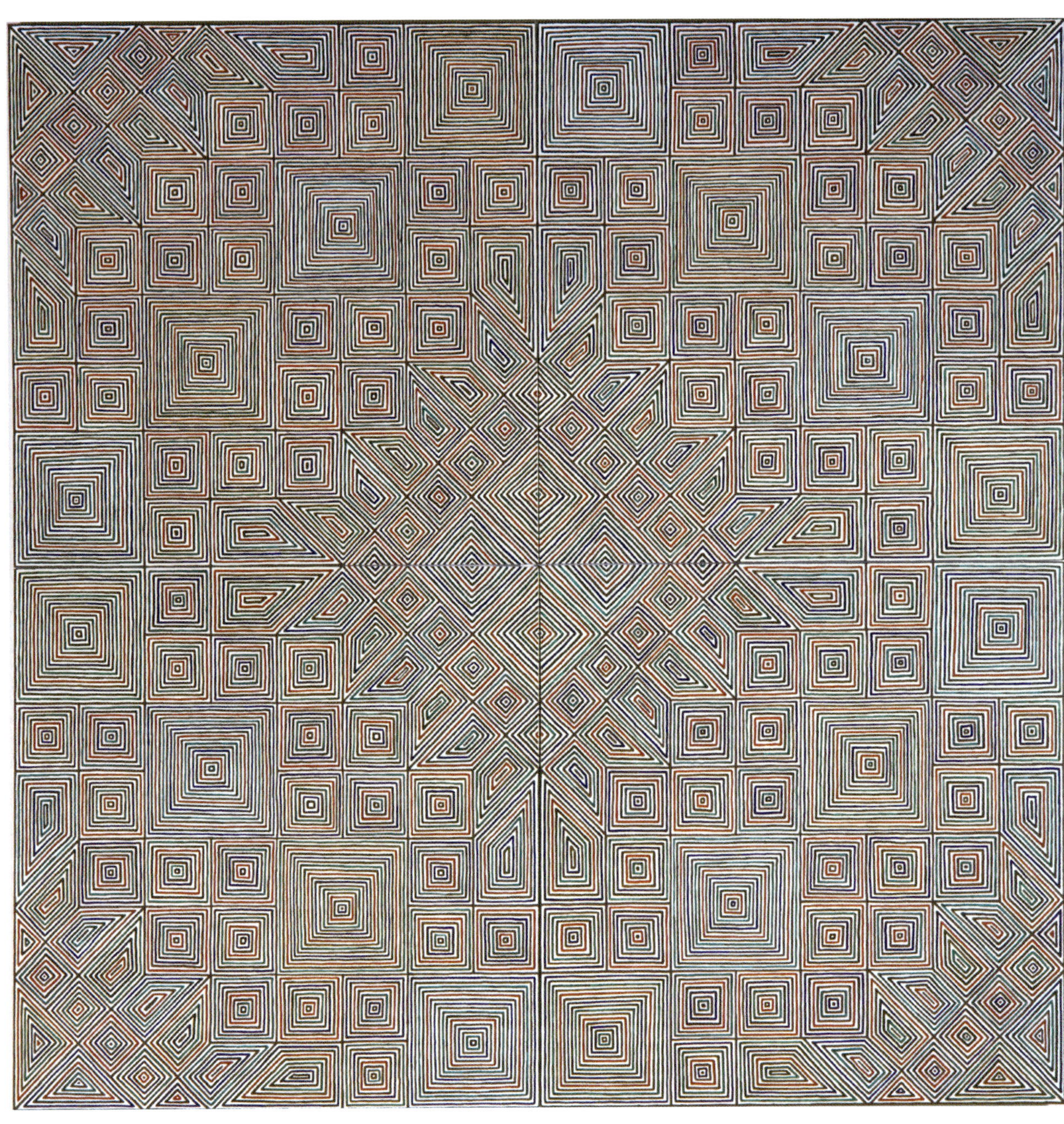

Primal OP 8′ x 8′ #1, 2004, acrylic on canvas, 8 x 8 ft.

Richard Elliott

Class of 1971

Since graduating from Central Washington University, Richard Elliott has created numerous public art commissions, and has also exhibited in hundreds of juried and solo exhibitions across the Pacific Northwest. In 2007 he received the prestigious Governor's Arts Award, chosen by Governor Christine Gregoire and the Washington State Arts Commission.

"The work that I have become best known for is monumental public art and the co-creation of the art site, Dick and Jane's Spot. However, my studio work has continued to evolve over the thirty-five-year span since graduating from CWU in 1971," Elliott said.

Some of Elliott's public commissioned pieces have been installed in the Belleview Light Rail Station in Denver, Colorado, the Municipal Parking Garage in Renton, Washington, and the Seattle-Tacoma International Airport. Although his public artwork consists primarily of large pieces crafted from industrial reflectors, his most recent studio works are paintings with intricate geometric designs.

Recent Career Highlights

- 2006: Solo exhibit at Bela Perla Gallery, Portland, Oregon
- 2006: Solo exhibit at Larson Gallery, Yakima, Washington
- 2000: Solo exhibit at Maryhill Museum of Art, Maryhill, Washington

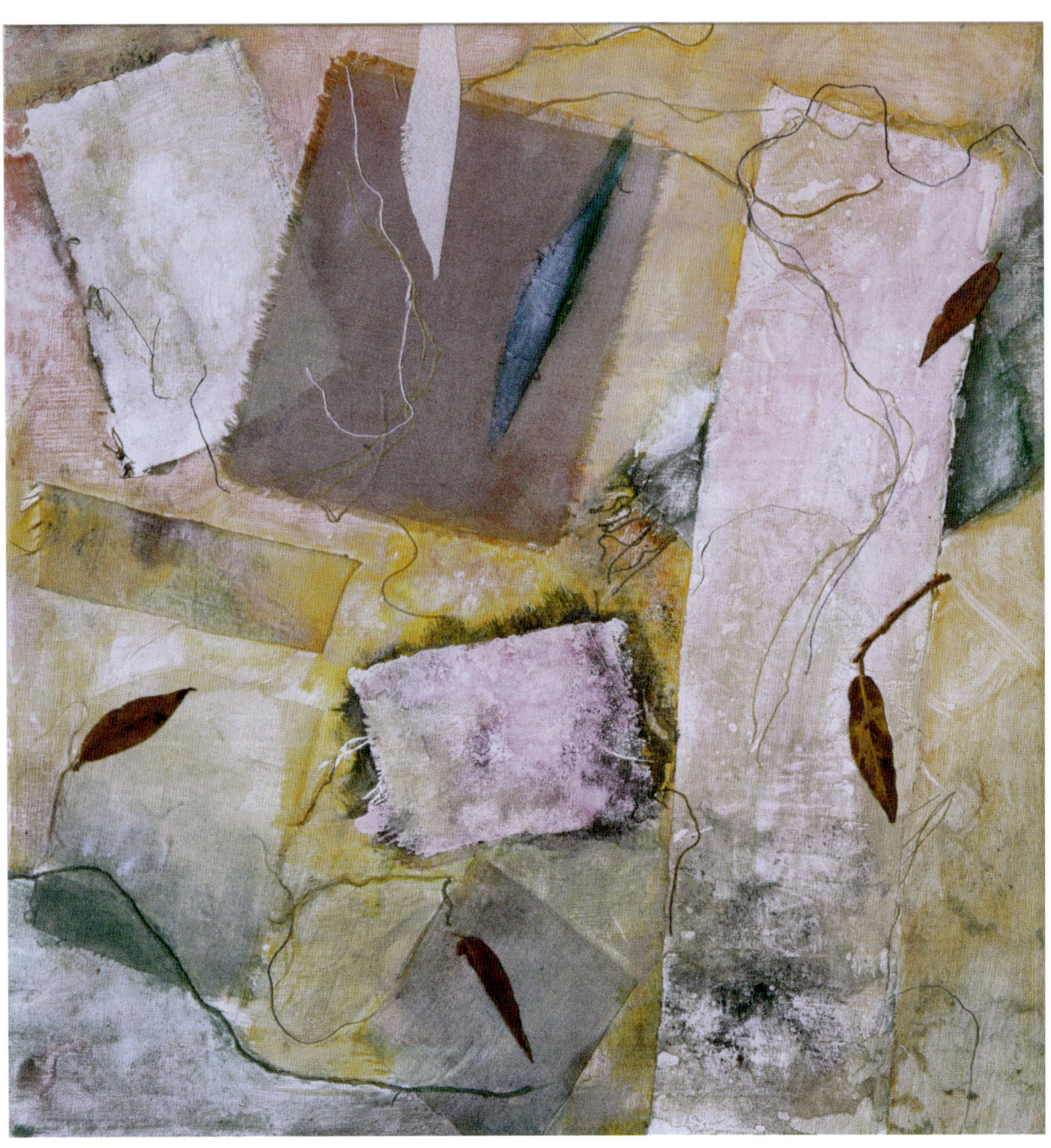

Heirloom Leaves, 2007, mixed media on board, 10¼ x 10½ in.

Sher Foster

Class of 1975

Ketchum, Idaho painter Sher Foster has created commissions for portraits and landscape scenes in oil, acrylic, and chalk since graduating from Central Washington University.

"The elements of dance and movement play an integral part in my pieces, and I am fascinated by sculptural and biomorphic shapes and forms," Foster said. "These elements are incorporated in my paintings using torn or cut pieces of fine silk fabric."

From 1991 to the present, Foster has participated in several group and solo exhibits, primarily in Idaho. She's also been busy teaching art, and has traveled extensively to exhibit her work.

"I have held workshops in the Middle East and Hawaii, and choreographed and produced stage productions at the Hilton Hawaiian Village and Ala Moana hotels in Honolulu."

Recent Career Highlights

- 2006: College of Southern Idaho solo exhibition, Hailey, Idaho
- 2006: Art in the Garden group exhibit, Hailey, Idaho
- 2006: Bungalow group exhibit, Hailey, Idaho

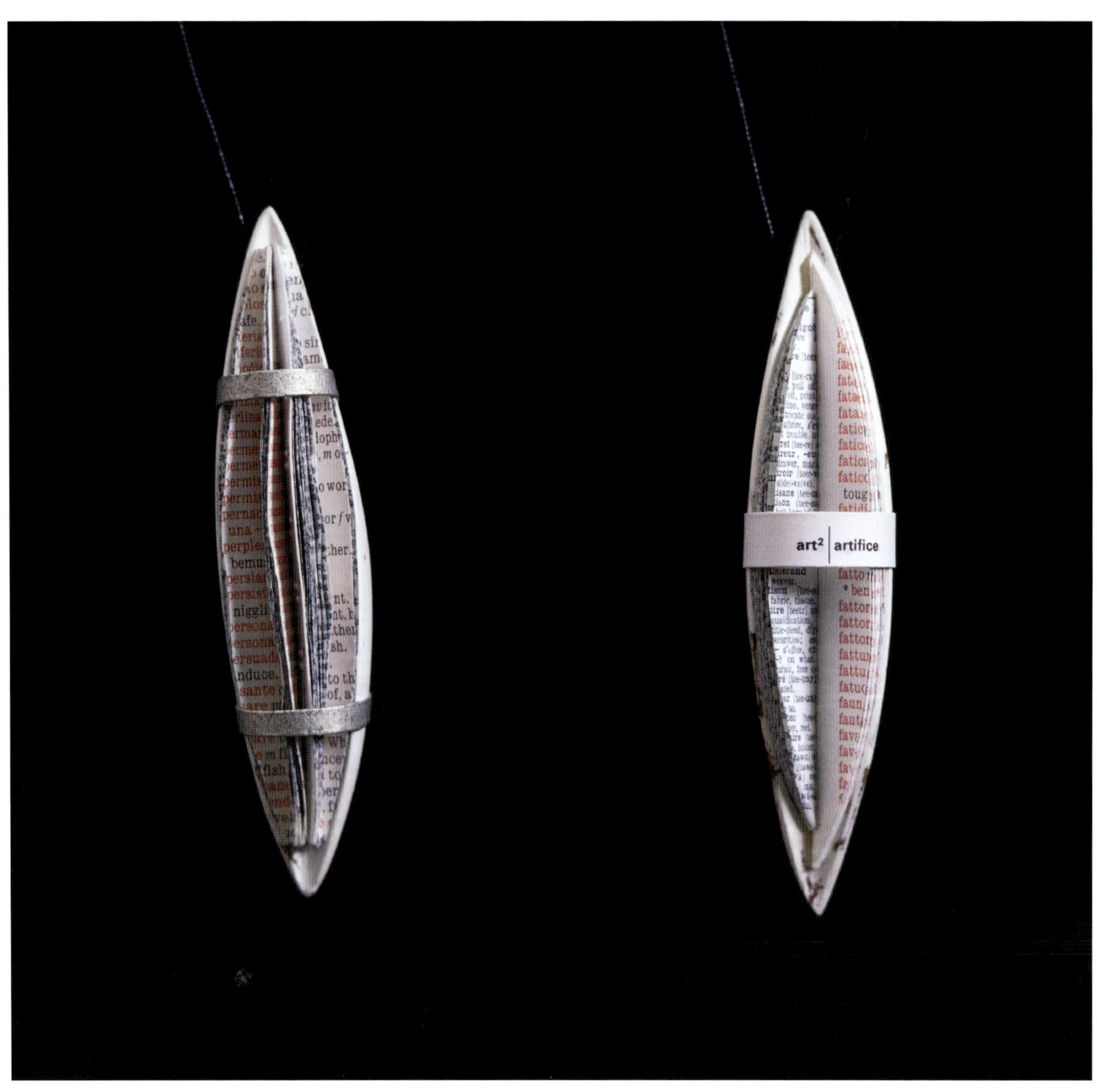

Both pieces by Bobbi Goodboy and Lois Harbaugh
Left: *C D E F G*, 2007, paper, plaster, dictionary, 1 x 5½ in.
Right: *Art 2*, 2007, paper, plaster, dictionary, 1 x 5½ in.

Bobbi Goodboy

Class of 1966

Painter Bobbi Goodboy has spent a great deal of time perfecting her skills in the chine collé technique, which she uses to create layered collages.

"It allows for the making of art in a nomadic lifestyle. My art can be rolled up and reestablished much like backpacking equipment. Each workday I unroll my backpack—layers of painted surfaces in rich relationships. A final finish is often given to the work using encaustic methods," Goodboy said.

In addition to her collages, Goodboy creates installations, free-hanging pieces, and book format work, such as paper jewelry.

Goodboy also works as an arts events coordinator, and co-founded Art Break Inc., a group that has hosted art-making events for several clients in the Seattle, Washington area.

Recent Career Highlights:

- 2007: Group exhibit, Pulp Function, Fuller Crafts Museum, Brockton, Massachusetts
- 2006: Solo exhibit, Mineral Gallery, Tacoma, Washington
- 2005: Group exhibit, Looking Forward, Glancing Back: Northwest Designer Craftsman at 50, Contemporary Crafts Gallery, Portland, Oregon

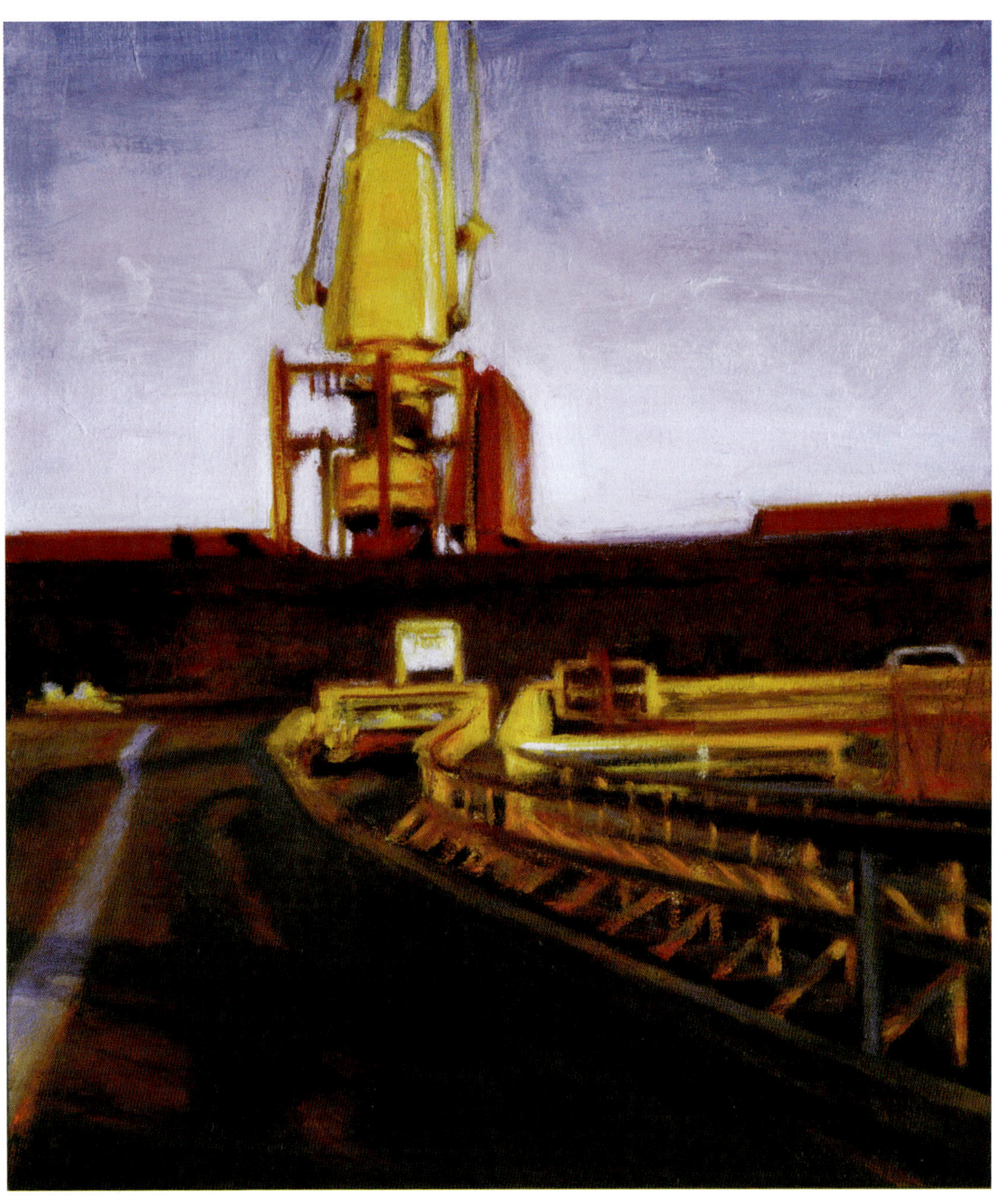

Cargo Ships 143, 2001, oil on canvas, 21 x 24 in.

Linda Grebmeier

Class of 1975 and 1978

Over the years, Linda Grebmeier has changed the focus of her paintings from the natural landscape to the urban, industrial scenes of Benicia, California.

Her studio in Benicia and its surroundings have inspired her new subject matter over the past eleven years.

"The industrial environment of my Benicia studio on the Carquinez Straight has changed the imagery of my art work," she said. "Prior to that move, I painted the light in the natural landscape in California, Oregon, and Washington."

Grebmeier graduated from Central Washington University with a bachelor's degree in fine arts and a master's degree in painting and drawing. She also taught printmaking and drawing at CWU from 1977 to 1978.

"Now I find another change occurring," she said. "A move from a regional identifiable landscape to an atmospheric, internal landscape of space and form."

Recent Career Highlights

- 2007: Commissioned artwork for label design, Imagery Estate Winery, Glen Ellen, California
- 2007: Guest artist instructor in painting, Arts Benicia Gallery Education Program, Benicia, California
- 2006: Wet Paint Invitational, live auction artist, Sonoma Valley Museum of Art, Sonoma, California

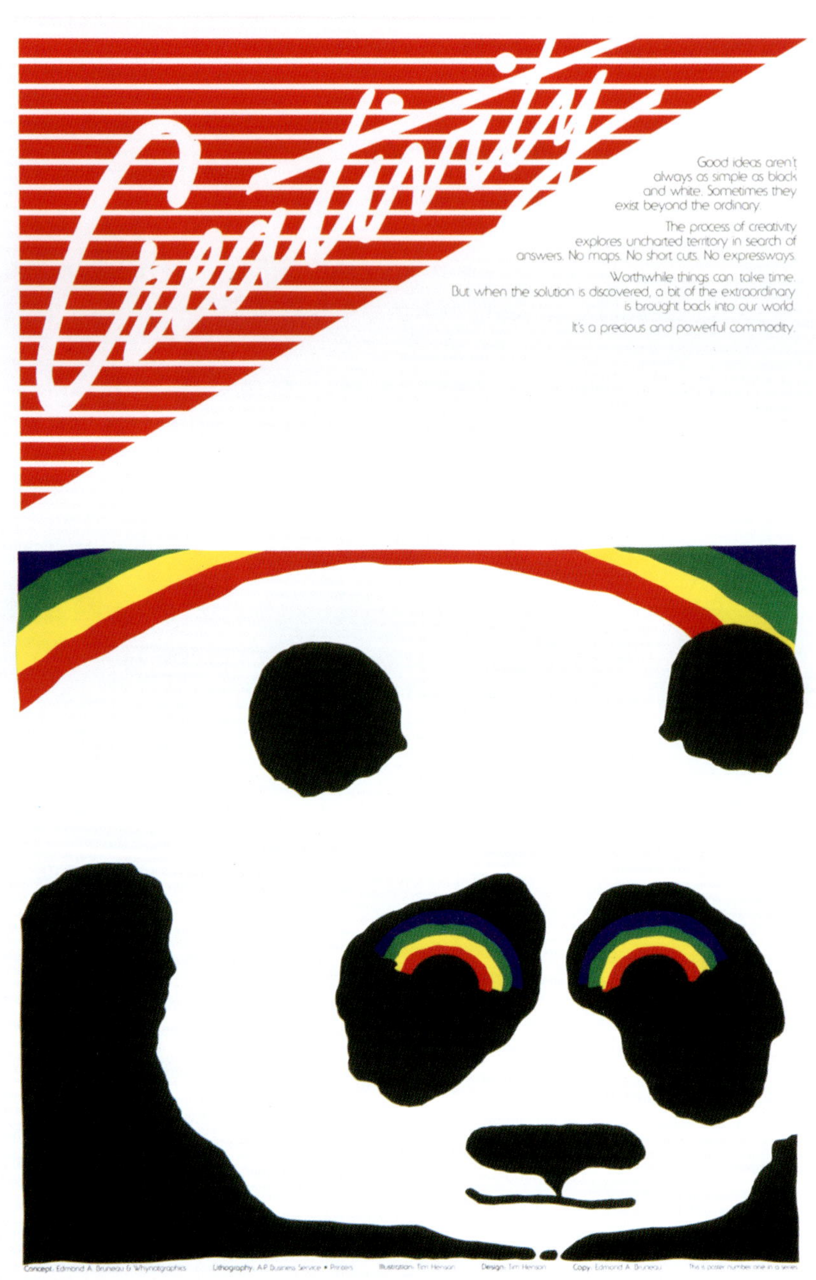

Creativity, 1982, cut Amberlith®, 15 x 22 in.

Tim Henson

Class of 1975

Since graduating with a bachelor of arts degree from Central Washington University, Tim Henson, a Spokane, Washington resident, has spent time working as a graphic designer and drafter.

In the mid-1970s, Henson worked as an artist and also served as treasurer for a Spokane City Council race. Recently he has worked for ASC Machine Tools, Inc. in Spokane, where he took a newly created position with the company's engineering department. He also spends time on artwork for companies such as the Rock Placing Company in Idaho, which hires him to create items such as holiday greeting cards.

"My career has changed focus over the years. I now support my family in the engineering field. I continue my creative endeavors as a freelance artist," Henson said.

As a freelancer, he focuses on interior design, signs, business cards, and sculpture.

Recent Career Highlights

- 1997 to present: ASC Machine Tools, Inc., Spokane, Washington
- 1983-1997: Advanced Input Devices, Coeur d' Alene, Idaho
- 1982: ISC Systems Corporation, Spokane, Washington

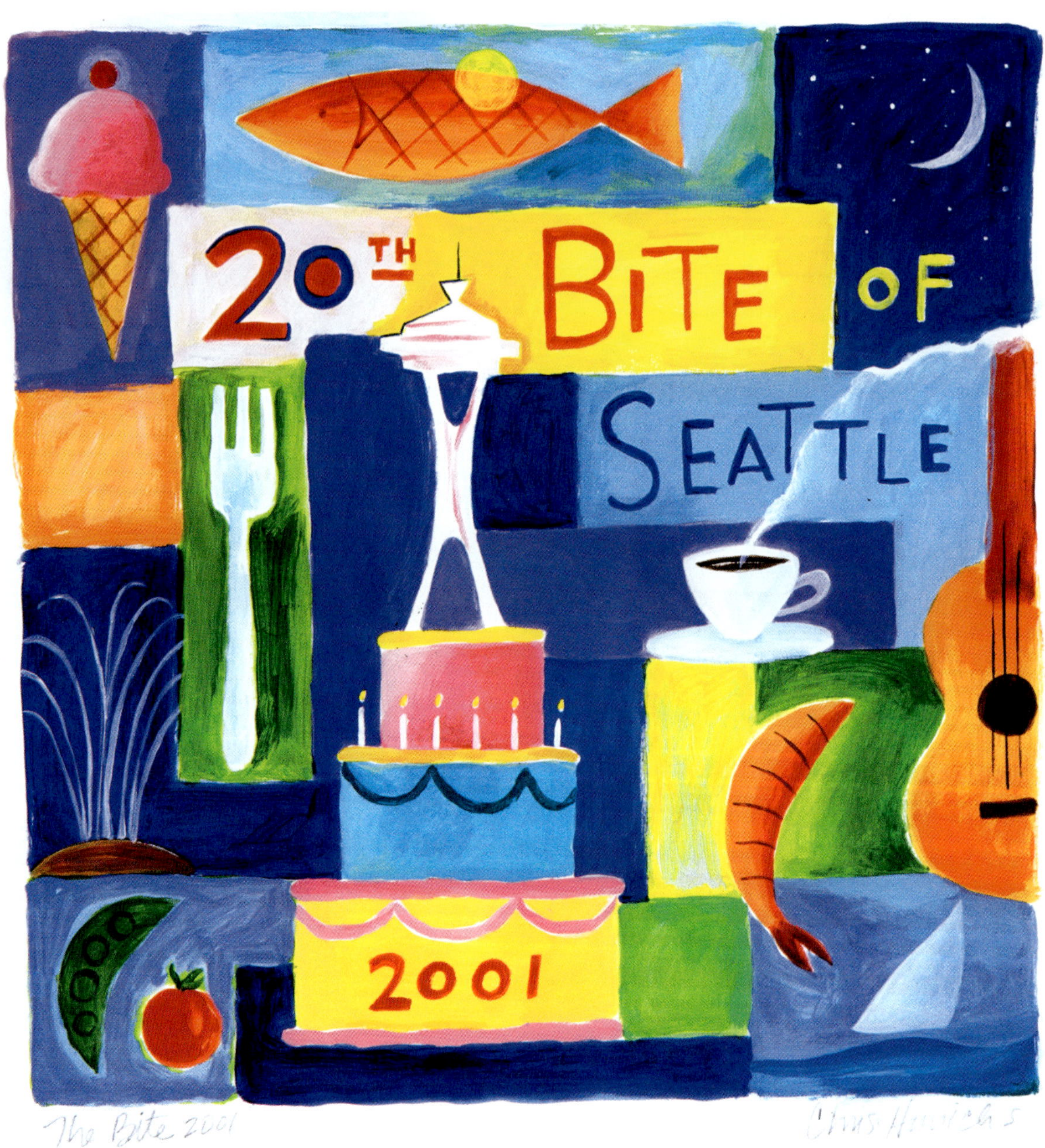

Bite of Seattle, 2001, acrylic on paper, 15¾ x 16¾ in.

Chris Hinrichs

Class of 1976

Chris Hinrichs, a Leavenworth, Washington resident, has spent her career working as a commercial illustrator since graduating from Central Washington University.

Companies and organizations use her designs, including Time Life Books, Stemilt Growers, Get Fit Foods, Seattle Folklife Festival, Bite of Seattle, and the City of Tacoma Chamber of Commerce.

"As a commercial illustrator and designer, I sell my visual style but the subject matter in my images is always determined by the project I have been hired to do," Hinrichs said. "Bold use of color is always part of my work. I paint with acrylics, but also create some of my work on the computer."

When not creating commercial art, Hinrichs is an adjunct instructor of illustration at Central Washington University.

Recent Career Highlights

- 2005: Created four banner designs that are on display in Tacoma, Washington's downtown district
- 1993-1999: Operated a graphic design firm specializing in package design for the food industry
- 1986-1993: Designer and project manager for Nordstrom's private food and cosmetic packaging labels

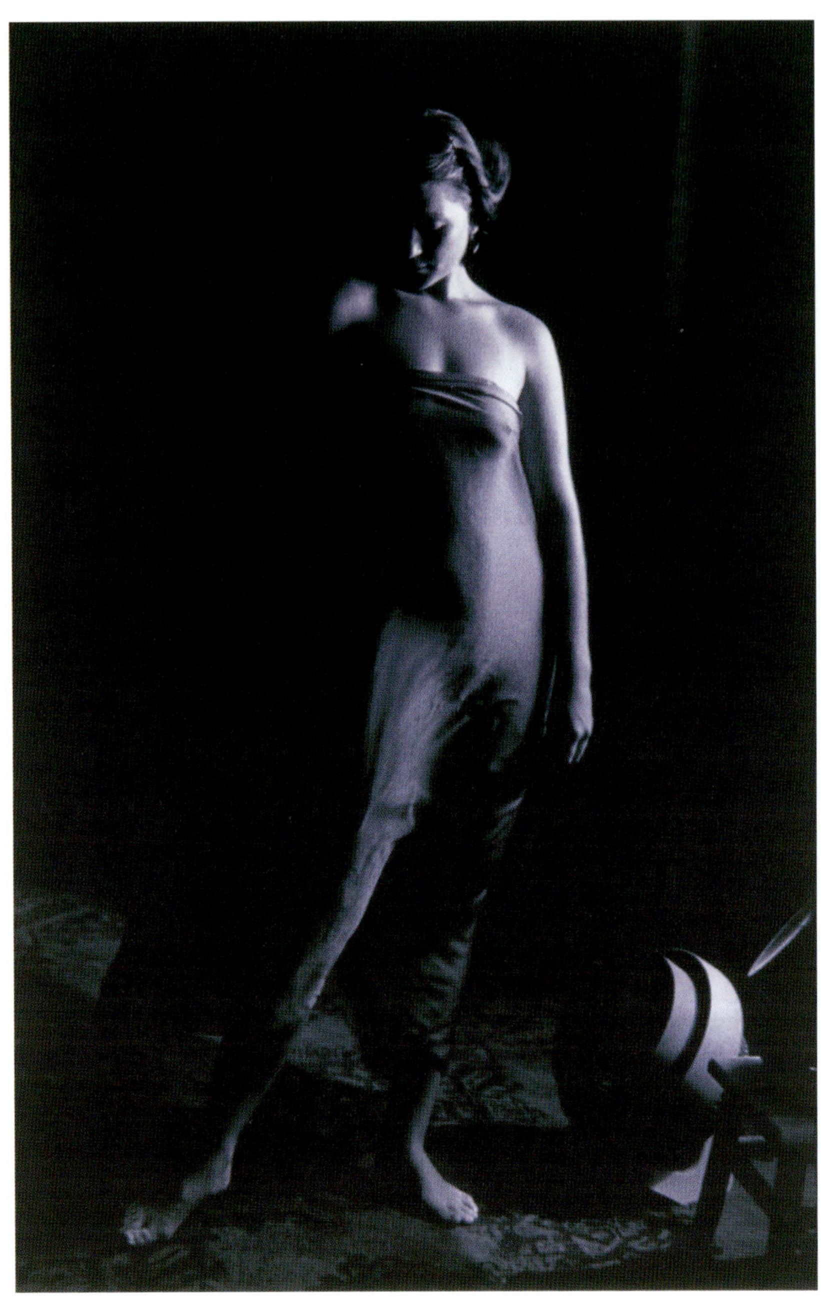

"Yet like Air," 2006, silver gelatin photograph, 7¾ x 12 in.

Marlene Hodge

Class of 1972

Artist Marlene Hodge graduated from Central Washington University with a commercial art degree, and has spent her career working primarily as a photographer. She also puts her artistic abilities to work as an instructional and classroom support technician for the art department at Centralia College in Centralia, Washington.

Hodge has exhibited her work throughout the Northwest, and plans to continue pursuing photography, which she has come to love, she said.

"At this time, I am enjoying photography immensely; looking, capturing, developing, and producing," she said. "One of the best aspects of photography is the ability to daydream in the midst of creating an image."

Over the years, Hodge has won several awards and been published in numerous photography books.

"During most of regular life, my brain is constantly talking to me, making lists, and planning. Photography takes me back to childhood, when I could unfocus my brain," she said.

Recent Career Highlights

- 2007: Olympia Arts Walk participant, Olympia, Washington
- 2004, 2003, and 2002: Finalist for *Photographer's Forum* magazine, Best of College Photography
- 2003, 2001, and 2000: Published in the literary and visual arts journal, *Beyond Parallax*

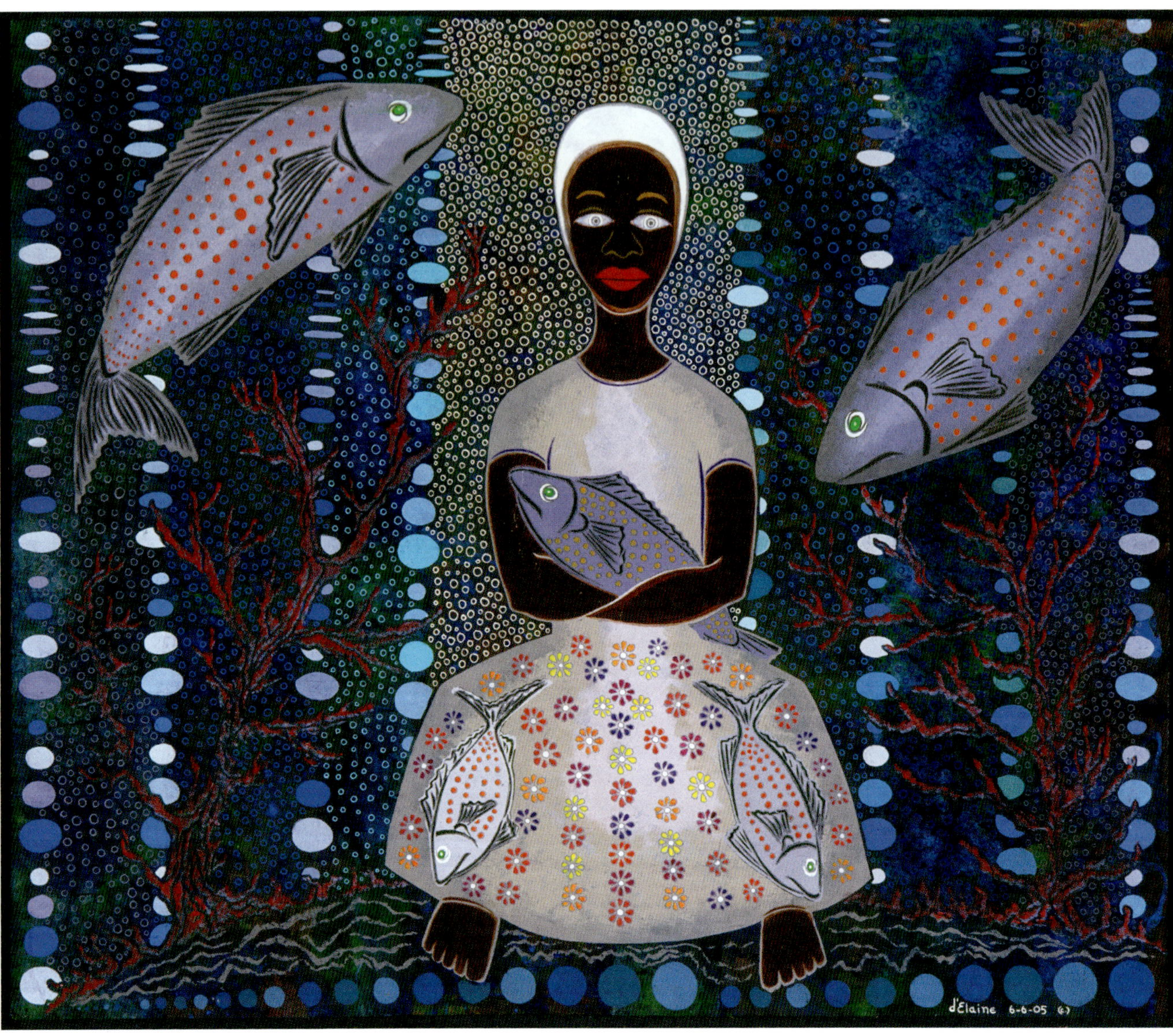

Beneath the Waves, 2005, acrylic on canvas, 36 x 30 in.

d'Elaine Ann Herard Johnson

Class of 1954

Edmonds, Washington resident d'Elaine Ann Herard Johnson has experienced a fulfilling career as not only a successful artist and teacher, but also as an exhibition juror, public servant, and founder of two organizations. In the 1970s, she founded the Mount Olympus Preserve for the Arts, and in 1997, she re-established the South Snohomish County Arts Roundtable, Snohomish, Washington.

Her own artwork focuses around water, myths, and ancient sea cultures.

"During the 1970s and continuing to the present, my inspiration has been the world of sea cultures of the past. My marine icons are enlivened through documentation of ancient myths and lore. Joseph Campbell has remained one of my major influences for interpreting mythologies for my writings, which accompany my paintings," she said.

A prolific artist, Johnson has participated in more than 600 exhibitions since the 1950s.

Recent Career Highlights:

- 1970-present: American Council for the Arts member
- 2005: Abilities Festival, juried exhibition of artists from eight countries, Toronto, Ontario, Canada
- 2004: VAS Fellow Exhibition, twelve artists chosen from sixty countries, United Nations Headquarters, New York, New York

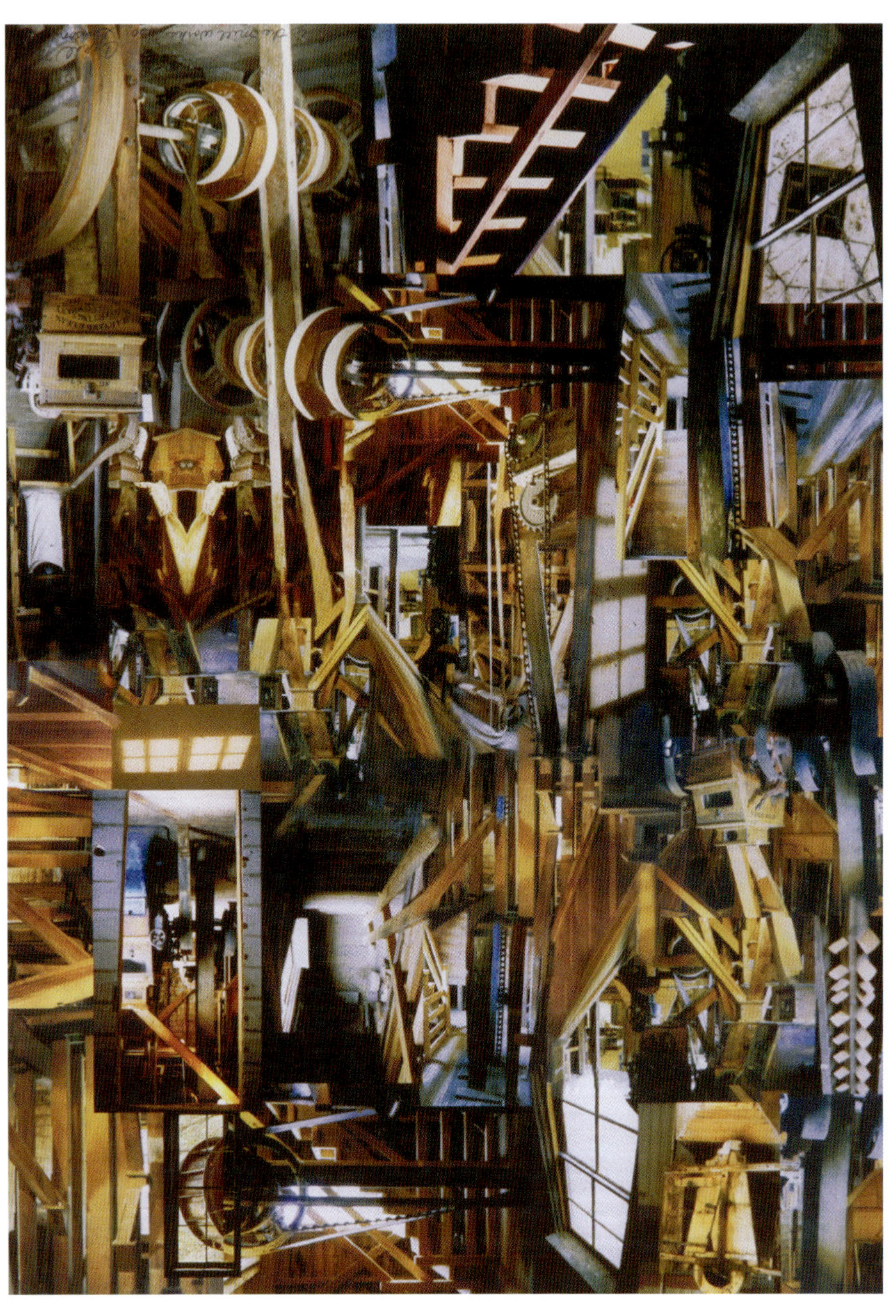

Inside the Millworks, 2001, photo collage, 15½ x 16¾ in.

Carol Johnson (Genson)

Class of 1965 and 2001

Ellensburg, Washington resident and artist Carol Johnson has spent her life teaching art and participating in local and regional art events.

In the unincorporated town of Thorp, Washington, she has worked as the school district's art and computer coordinator, art educator, and led the high school's yearbook and newspaper. Her efforts as an art educator have not gone unnoticed.

"Throughout my teaching career, my students have represented Ellensburg School District and central Washington in the Washington State High School Art Show by winning the top awards," Johnson said. "Several works by my students have been selected as one of seven to go to Olympia to compete with approximately 16,000 other high school students for the state's top seven awards."

In 1965 she earned a bachelor's degree in art education from Central Washington University. In 2001, she returned to Central where she obtained a master's degree in education.

Recent Career Highlights

- 1984-present, Ellensburg Community Television producer, Ellensburg, Washington
- 2005 and 2006: Paint Ellensburg artist participant, Ellensburg, Washington
- 1965-1972 and 1979-2006: Thorp School District art and computer instructor, Thorp, Washington

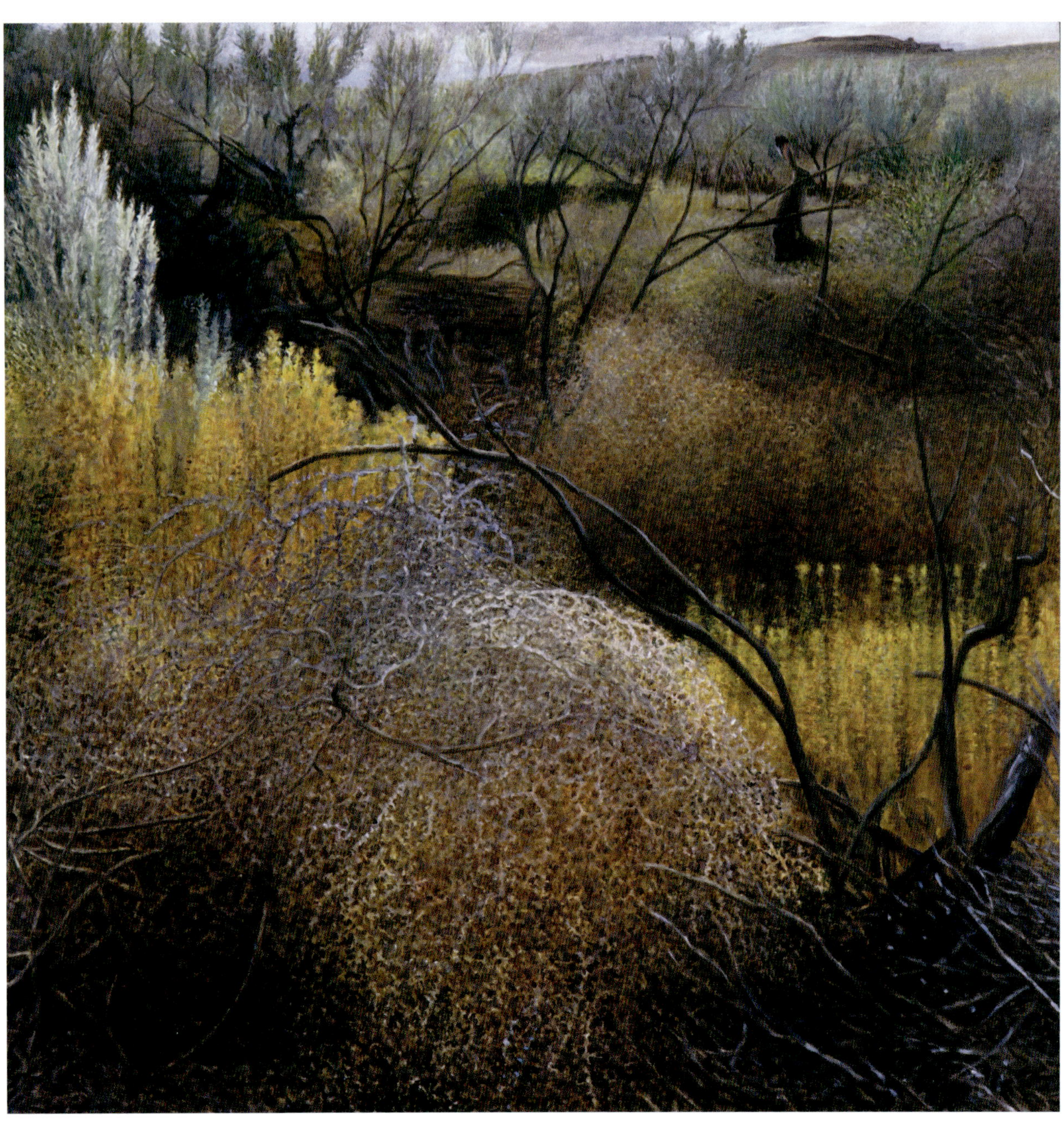

Jackrabbit's Domain, 2006, acrylic on canvas, 36 x 36 in.

Roger L. Jones

Class of 1964

Since 1988, painter Roger Jones has exhibited his work at the Linda Hodges Gallery in Seattle, Washington. Born in Ellensburg, Washington, his paintings often capture the rural, rolling hills of eastern Washington. Presently, Jones lives in Mountlake Terrace, Washington.

"My love and respect for the natural world is reflected in my paintings of landscapes, incorporating plants and animals in realistic compositions," he said.

After graduating from Central Washington University in 1964 with a bachelor's degree in Education, Jones taught art classes in the Edmonds School District in Edmonds, Washington, from 1964 to 1967. In 1972, Jones received his master's degree in fine arts at the University of Washington. He also taught at the Factory of Visual Art in Seattle and the Bellevue Art Museum School throughout the 1970s.

In 1996 he received a commission from Central Washington University to create paintings for the university's Science Building.

Recent Career Highlights:

- 2007: Solo exhibit, Linda Hodges Gallery, Seattle, Washington
- 1999-2000: Boeing illustrator, Bellevue, Washington
- 1999: Group exhibit, Washington Landscapes, Simon Edwards Gallery, Yakima, Washington

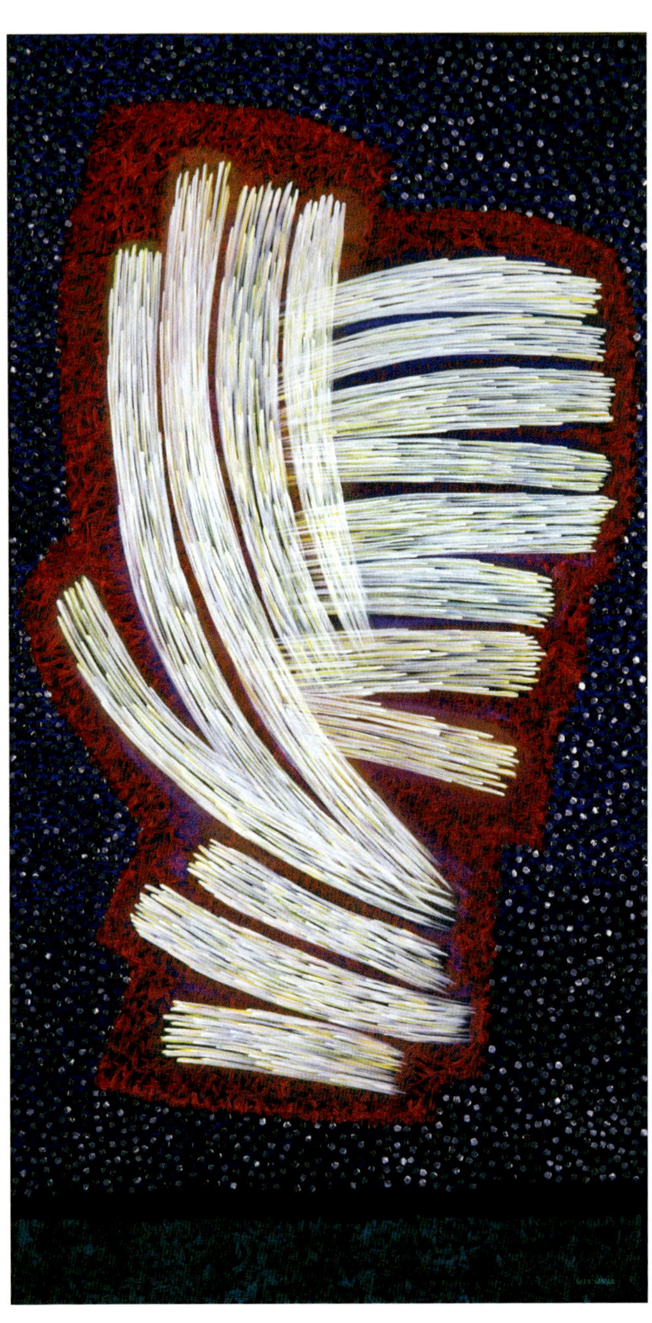

Untitled, 2006, acrylic and nails on canvas,
31¾ x 59¾ in.

Glen LaMar

Class of 1963

Painter Glen LaMar's work conveys strong spiritual and biblical themes, without, as the artist stated, being "illustrative or trite."

"I have been especially intrigued with the use of symbolism to represent the human soul (or spirit) and God's presence," LaMar said. "While I have painted a variety of subject matters not limited to religious subjects, that has been my prevailing personal interest."

Much of LaMar's work is very natural and organic in form. He lives in Olympia, Washington, and has studied at several schools, including the Art Student's League in New York City and the Banff School of Fine Arts in Banff, Alberta, Canada. In September 2006 he was one of four visual artists to be recognized and have his artwork published as part of a national competition held by *Ministry & Liturgy* magazine.

Recent Career Highlights:

- 2006: Featured exhibit at Capps Art Gallery, St. Martin's University, Lacey, Washington
- 2006: Juried exhibit at Springfield Art Association, Springfield, Illinois
- 2004: One-month residency at the Julia and David White Artist Colony, Ciudad Colón, Costa Rica

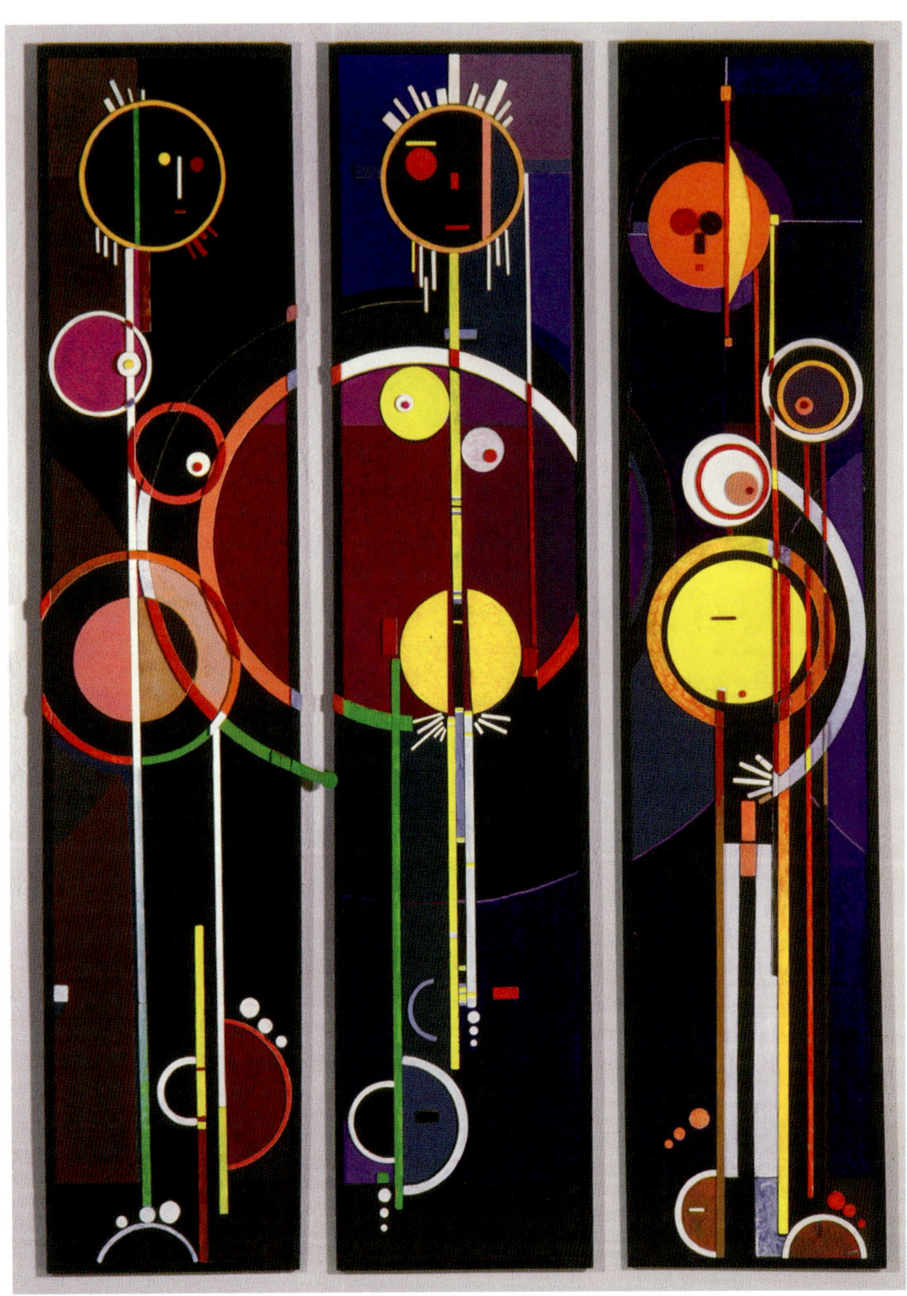

Three Graces, 2003, acrylic on board, 54½ x 78 in.

Marvin Lilley

Class of 1978

Arlington, Washington artist Marvin Lilley spends his days working in a studio, where he lives with friends. He focuses primarily on painting acrylic pieces, and recently worked on a series focusing on flowers.

"I mostly stay in my studio and try to keep up with the contemporary, experimental, and explorative," Lilley said. "I also try to figure myself out along the way."

Lilley's work tends to focus around the themes of symbolism, reality, faith, hope, and charity. He also takes an interest in crop circles, which he said have influenced his work for the past seven years.

Recent Career Highlights:

- *Black Panel Study*, a series of paintings focusing on symbolism
- *Three Graces*, a series of paintings focusing on faith, hope, and charity

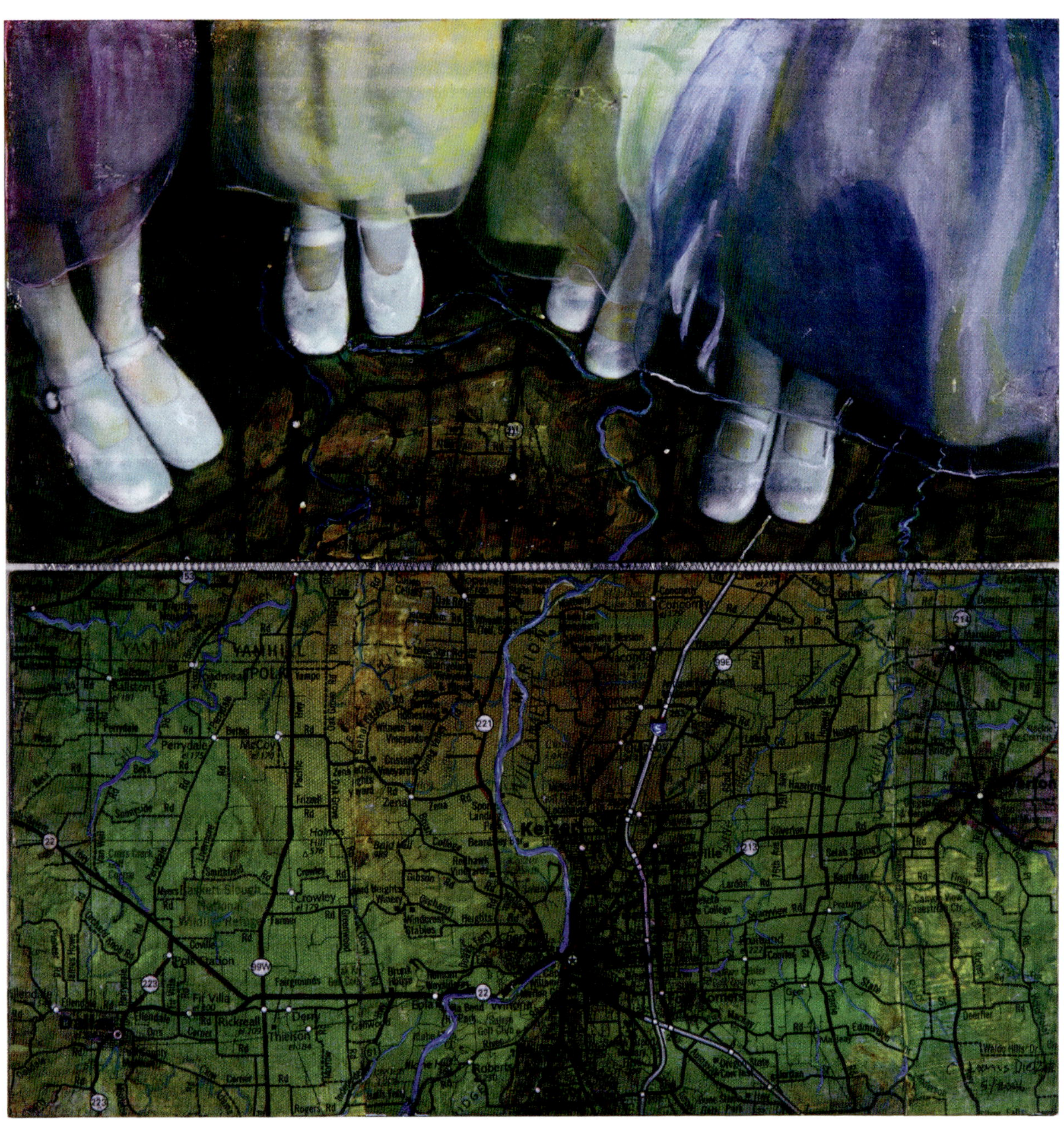

Standing in Place, 2006, acrylic on canvas, 16 x 16 in.

Corrine Loomis Dietz

Class of 1977

Salem, Oregon painter and photographer Corrine Loomis Dietz has taught more than 120 workshops across the Northwest on traditional and contemporary uses of acrylic paints. Many of her workshops have been through the company, Golden Artist Colors, Inc., a paint company she has been affiliated with since 1999.

"Golden has gifted me with extensive training, advancing my technical knowledge of pigments, binders, mediums, gels, grounds, and varnishes," Loomis Dietz said. "Through this affiliation and collaboration with my contemporaries, I have encountered vast resources to explore creative options."

Loomis Dietz focuses on photography and painting when she is not teaching. She uses her photos as canvases, where she applies transparent layers of acrylic paint, giving her images depth and vibrancy.

"A love of recording moments in time, examining color, problem solving, and teaching encompasses my life's work," she said. "With the blessings of time and application, I have gained recognition as a figurative artist and educator."

Recent career highlights:

- 2006: Oregon Art Annual second place award, Salem, Oregon
- 2006: Salem Art Association Kite Show, Salem, Oregon
- 2005: Borland Gallery Photographers Invitational, Silverton, Oregon

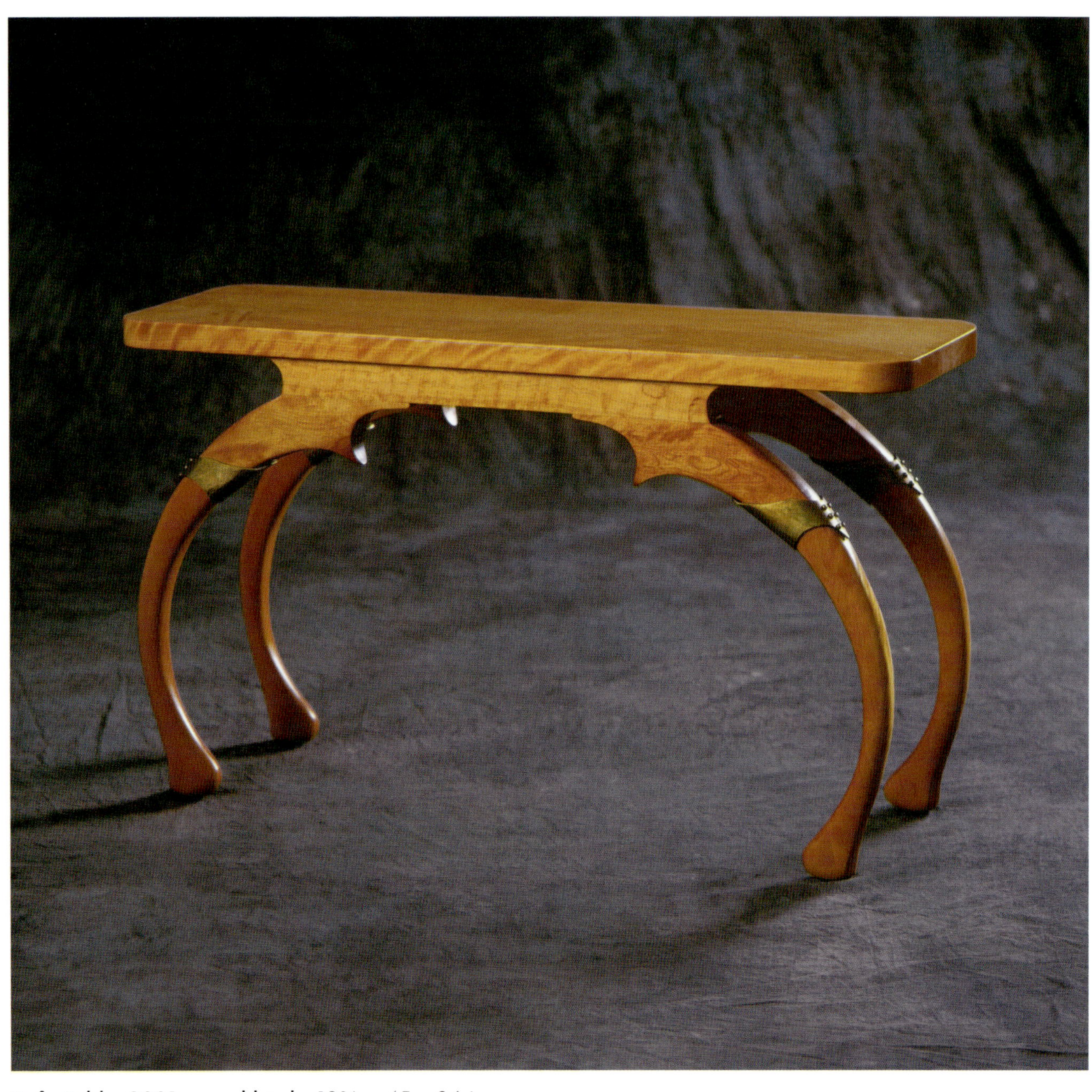

Sofa Table, 2001, wood birch, 13¾ x 45 x 26 in.

Lynn Louise

Class of 1974

Sculptor Lynn Louise, a Roslyn, Washington resident, focuses her work around specific materials, including laminated wood and bronze. Her work is organic and loosely based on the human figure.

"Even after all these years, I am in the process of becoming a sculptor working at becoming an artist," she said. "It is the mental and manual approach to woodworking that makes it completely satisfying. The development of art in wood is a measured, controlled, almost gentle endeavor."

Since 2004, Louise has been employed by the Bronze Works fine art foundry in Tacoma, Washington, where she has honed her casting skills by fabricating commercial sculpture.

"Working on numerous artists' works has broadened the depth of my skill and work. The greater source of inspiration, however, is my fellow employees, who are all artists themselves."

Recent Career Highlights

- 2004: The Works Gallery, Bronze Works foundry, Tacoma, Washington
- 2002: Two-woman exhibit, Hoodsport Winery & Gallery, Tacoma, Washington
- 1990: Women in Art juried exhibit, winner of the Tacoma/Pierce County YWCA sculpture award

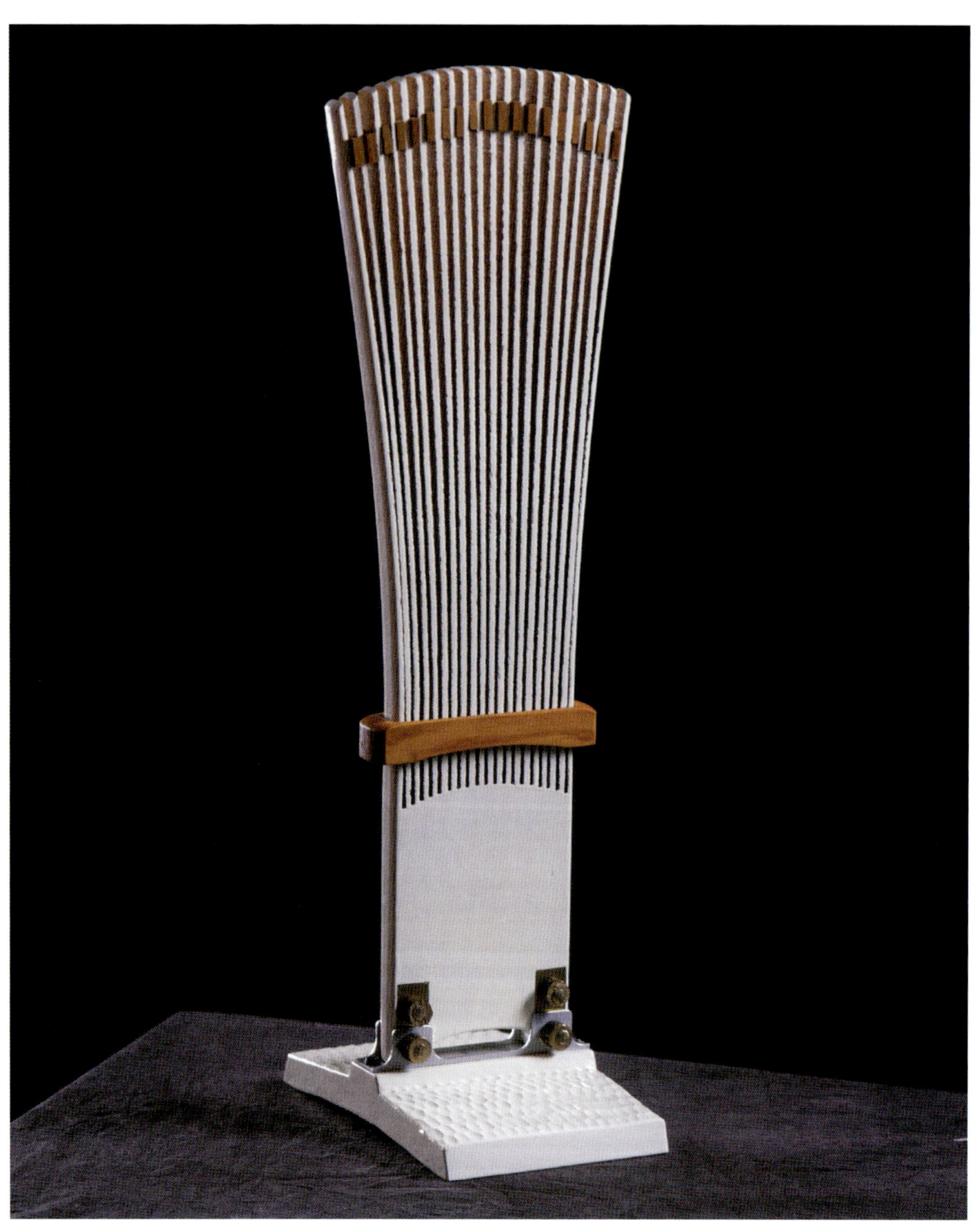

Pek Spoos, 2005, wood, metal, and paint, 7 x 4½ x 18¾ in.

Erik Maakestad

Class of 1979 and 1981

Since graduating from Central Washington University, sculptor Erik Maakestad has exhibited his artwork nationally, and is presently an associate professor at Hendrix College in Conway, Arkansas.

"From 1999 through most of 2004, I provided a significant level of leadership, as the Hendrix College of Arts Department changed almost every aspect of its presence on campus," Maakestad said. "We completely revamped the art major, our budget, and spending process."

Presently, he is working on a commissioned piece in Conway, Arkansas, where he is designing a large sculpture installation.

"I am working on an idea that could help humanize a site that needs some help," he said.

Maakestad splits his time between Arkansas and Stehekin, Washington. The vivacity of the South "combined with the calm, the beauty, and the beloved community that I enjoy in the Cascades has somehow become the motivating force behind most of my recent work," Maakestad observed.

Recent Career Highlights:

- 2008: Public art commission, the Harkrider Project, Conway, Arkansas
- 2006: Group exhibit, Water, Golden West Gallery, Stehekin, Washington
- 2005: The Big Show, Portal Mine Museum, Holden, Washington

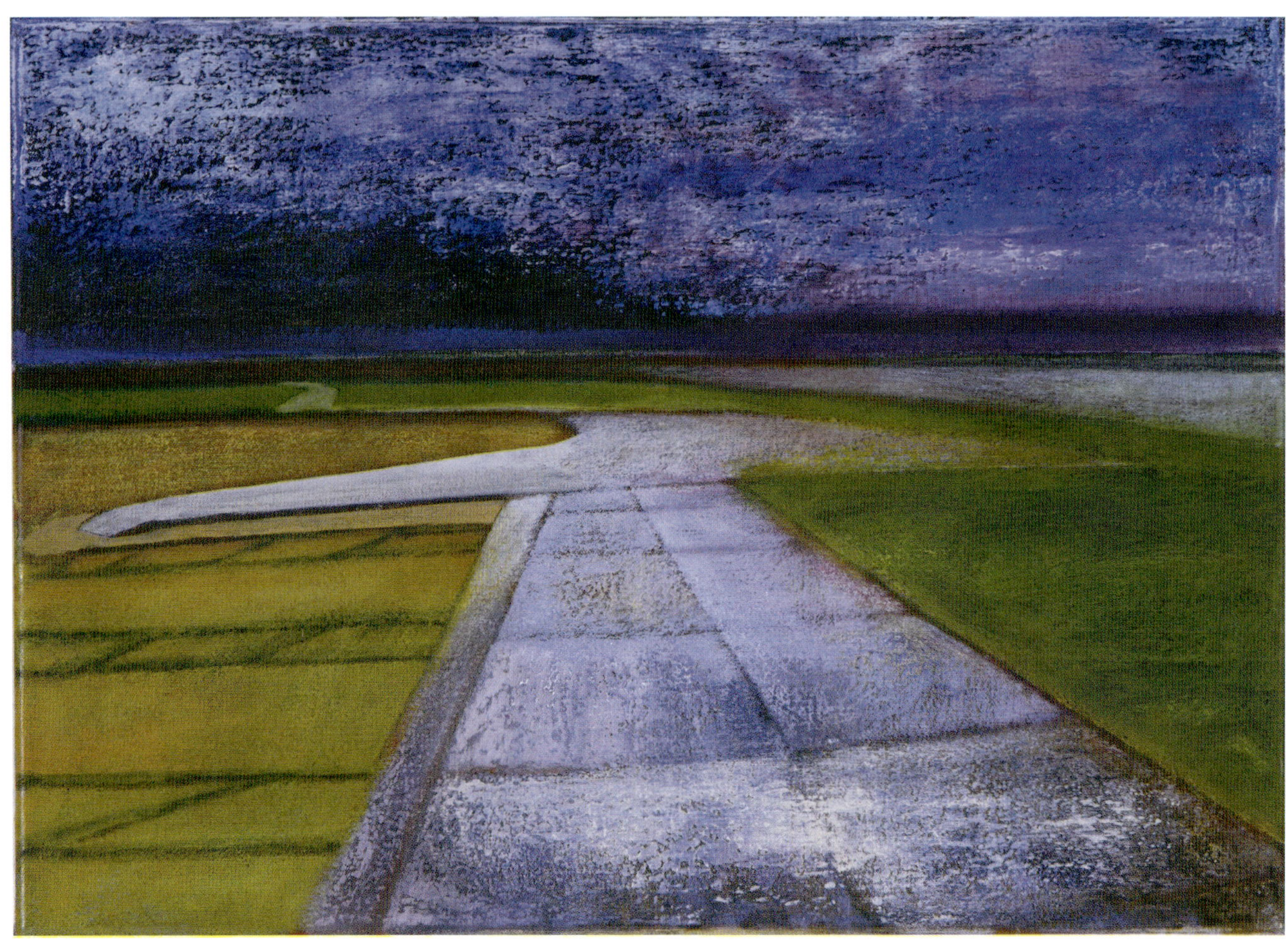

Sidewalk, 2004, oil on canvas, 20 x 14 in.

Susan (Ginalick) Maakestad

Class of 1979 and 1981

Painter Susan Maakestad has exhibited her work across the country since graduating from Central Washington University with bachelor and master of fine arts degrees. Her work was also featured in a 1995 quarterly edition of "New American Paintings," a juried exhibition-in-print.

The Memphis, Tennessee resident is fascinated with "spaces in between things, the unnoticed marginal spaces in the urban landscape," she said. "Likewise, as a painter, I like painting in that precarious place between abstraction and naturalism. I find inspiration in ordinary urban places such as parking lots and intersections."

Maakestad has also taught for several years, and is currently an associate professor at the Memphis College of Art. The city of Memphis strongly influences her art, she said.

"Memphis is both earthy and atmospheric. Here humidity and pollution turn air to mass. Heat waves dissolve substance. The river appears to be dense and slow yet is swift and deadly. I am searching for something to love in this urban scene even as I long for the consolations of nature."

Recent Career Highlights

- 2006: Solo exhibit, Clough-Hanson Gallery, Memphis, Tennessee
- 2006: Two-person exhibit, Perry Nicole Fine Art, Memphis, Tennessee
- 2000-2005: Awarded artist residencies in Georgia, Minnesota, Virginia, and Vermont

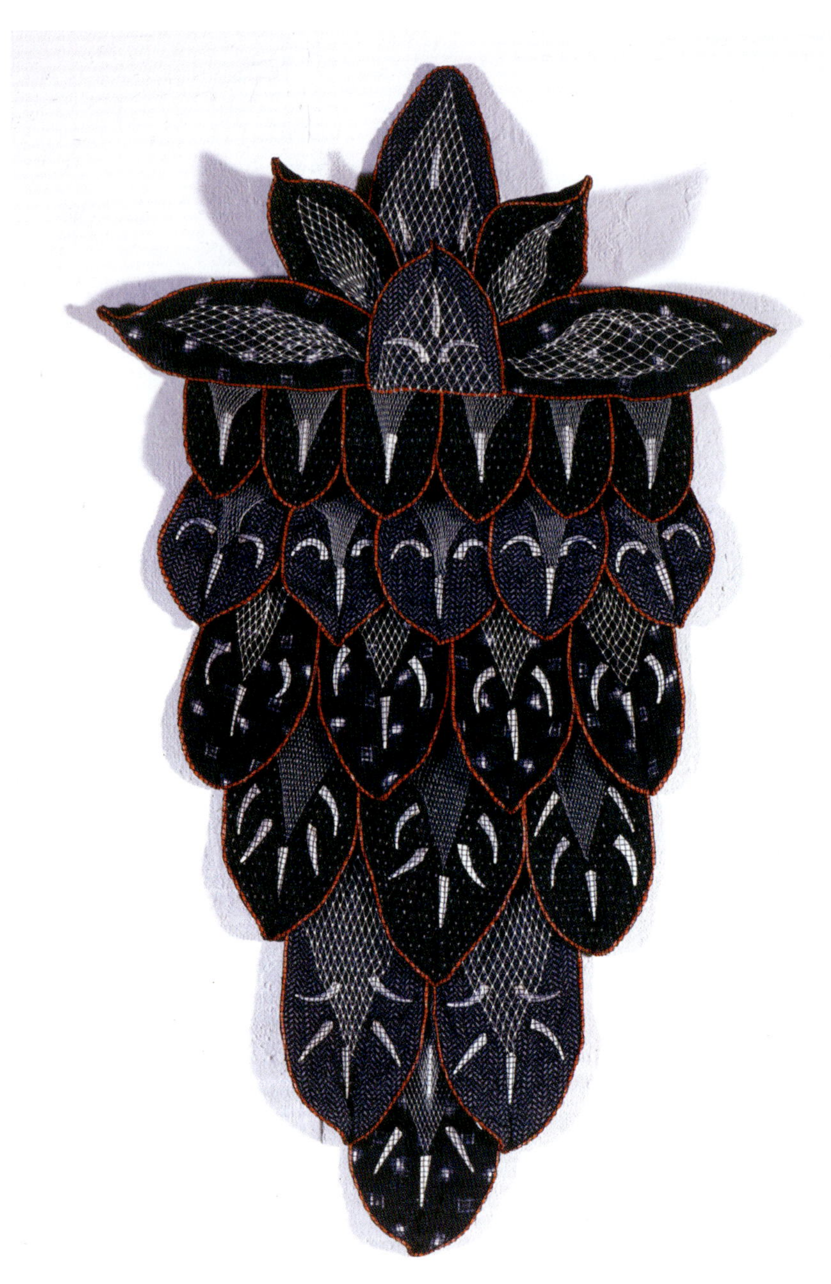

Fearless Symmetry, 2002, fiber, 30½ x 52 in.

Nancy MacKenzie

Class of 1956

Nancy MacKenzie's work, like that of most artists, has grown and changed over the years. Her major transformation as an artist began in 1983, when she took her first surface design workshop.

"I have always drawn, painted, and constructed things, but fiber art was not a concept in my college days. When I took my first surface design workshop, I began to see new possibilities for creating pattern on cloth which could become art, whether on the body, on the table, or on the wall," she said.

Her work quickly changed, and she found even more inspiration a year later when she took a workshop in *roketsu-zome*, which means wax and dye in Japanese. "When I could devote full time to my art, I began to make wearables that projected social commentary, and were more concerned with message than utility. Experimenting with only marginally wearable materials, such as barbed wire and baling twine, led me off of the body and onto the wall," she explained.

Since 1994, the Stillwater, Minnesota resident has worked as a self-employed artist, and has participated in several exhibits per year.

Recent Career Highlights:

- 2006: International juried exhibit, World of Wearable Art, the Events Centre, Wellington, New Zealand
- 2006: Featured in the publication, *American Craft*, August/September
- Member of Friends of Fiber Art International, Minnesota Crafts Council, Surface Design Association, and other related organizations

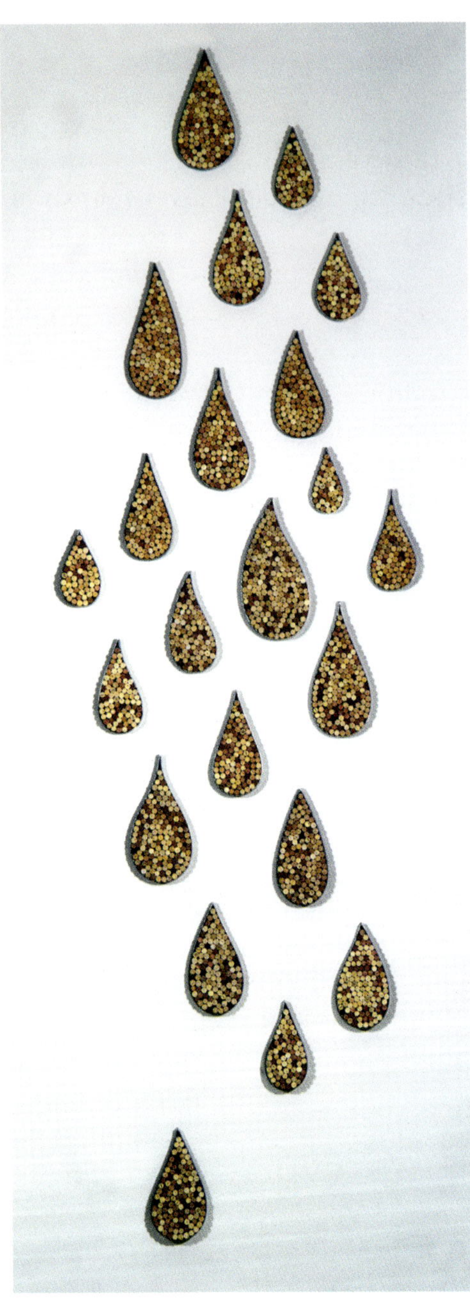

Blood, Sweat, and Tears,
2007, steel and wine corks,
variable 5 x 16 ft.

Gale McCall

Class of 1980

Gale McCall, an Inglewood, California resident, has accumulated a long list of public art installations throughout the West Coast, including several in California.

Her artwork, which consists of generally large metal sculptures, has been installed in libraries, hotels, rail stations, and other locations. She's also shown in dozens of solo and group exhibits.

"I research and work from written and visual sources that I collect for specific pieces and projects. My work reflects an intuitive commentary on orders and disorders in nature and the civilized world. It attempts to develop a narrative language that offers an alternative way of seeing what things are, were, or could be," McCall said.

McCall has also taught at several California schools, as well as in Zurich, Switzerland. Her most recent teaching post was at the Southern California Institute of Architecture in Los Angeles, where she taught community development design.

Recent Career Highlights:

- 2006: Former Ambassador Hotel site, historic mural commission for Los Angeles Unified School District, Los Angeles, California
- 2004: Cypress Park Library, commissioned digital mural, Los Angeles, California
- 2004: Lake Meridian Park project, commissioned sculptures, Kent, Washington

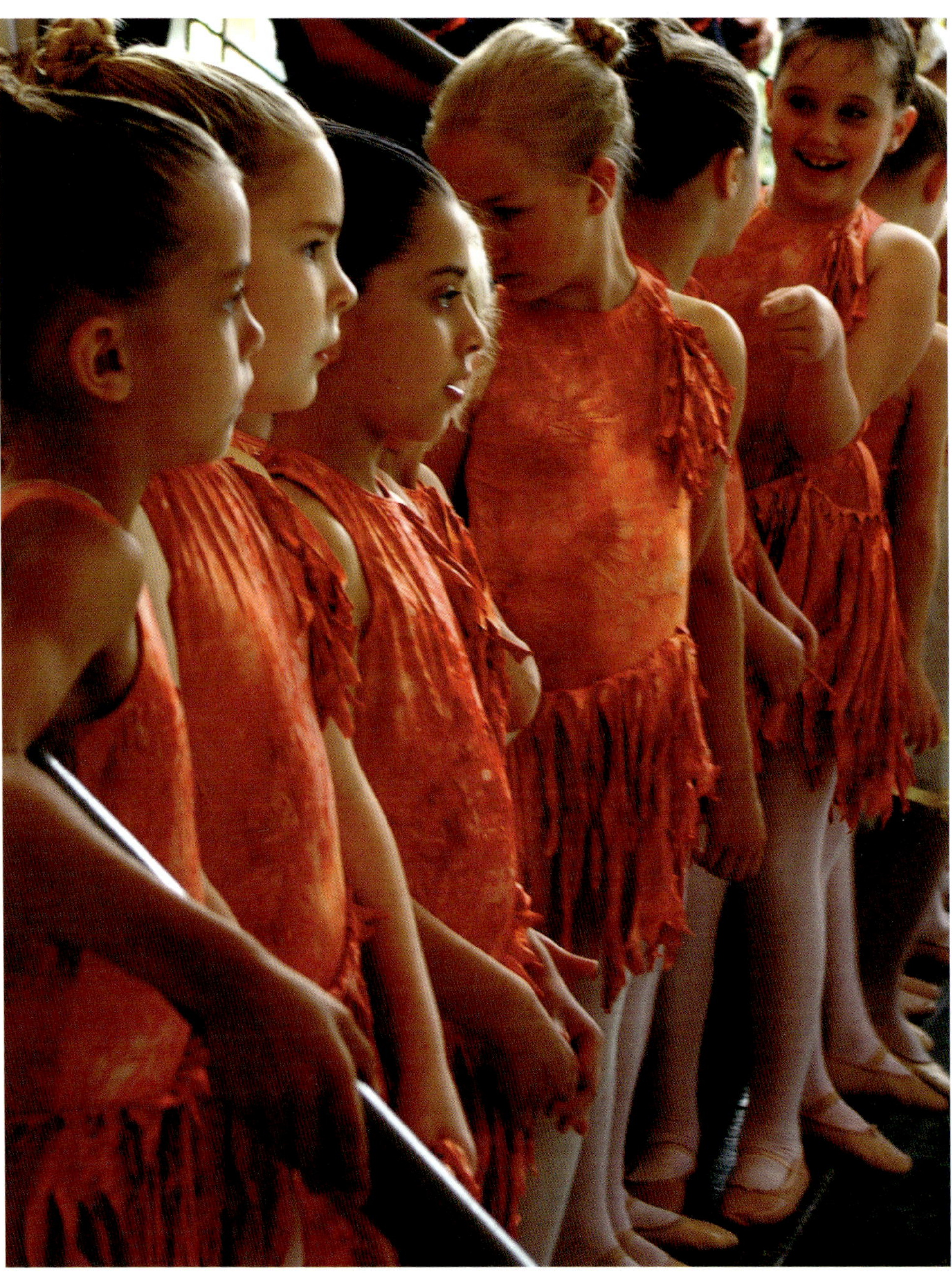

"All in a Row," 2007, digital photograph, 7½ x 9½ in.

Roberta McTimmons
Class of 1966

Roberta McTimmons, an Onalaska, Washington resident, spends most of her time working on her farm, where she tends to seven horses, along with several other animals. She also spends a good deal of time on photography.

"Excluding time spent working at an art museum and a radio/television station, my career path veered away from active participation in the art world. In 2004 I retired from a career with the state of Washington and now have time to explore a long-time interest in photography. I strive to record color and design via digital imagery," McTimmons said.

She exhibits her photography at various exhibits throughout the Northwest, including an exhibit in fall of 2007 in Longview, Washington.

Recent Career Highlights:

- 2006: Photography contest first place winner in the people category, honorable mention in animal category, McClelland Center, Longview, Washington
- 2006: Award-winning photo displayed during month-long exhibit, Longview Public Library, Longview, Washington
- 2005: Photography contest first place winner in the abstract category, Judge's Choice award, and third place in the scenic category, McClelland Center, Longview, Washington

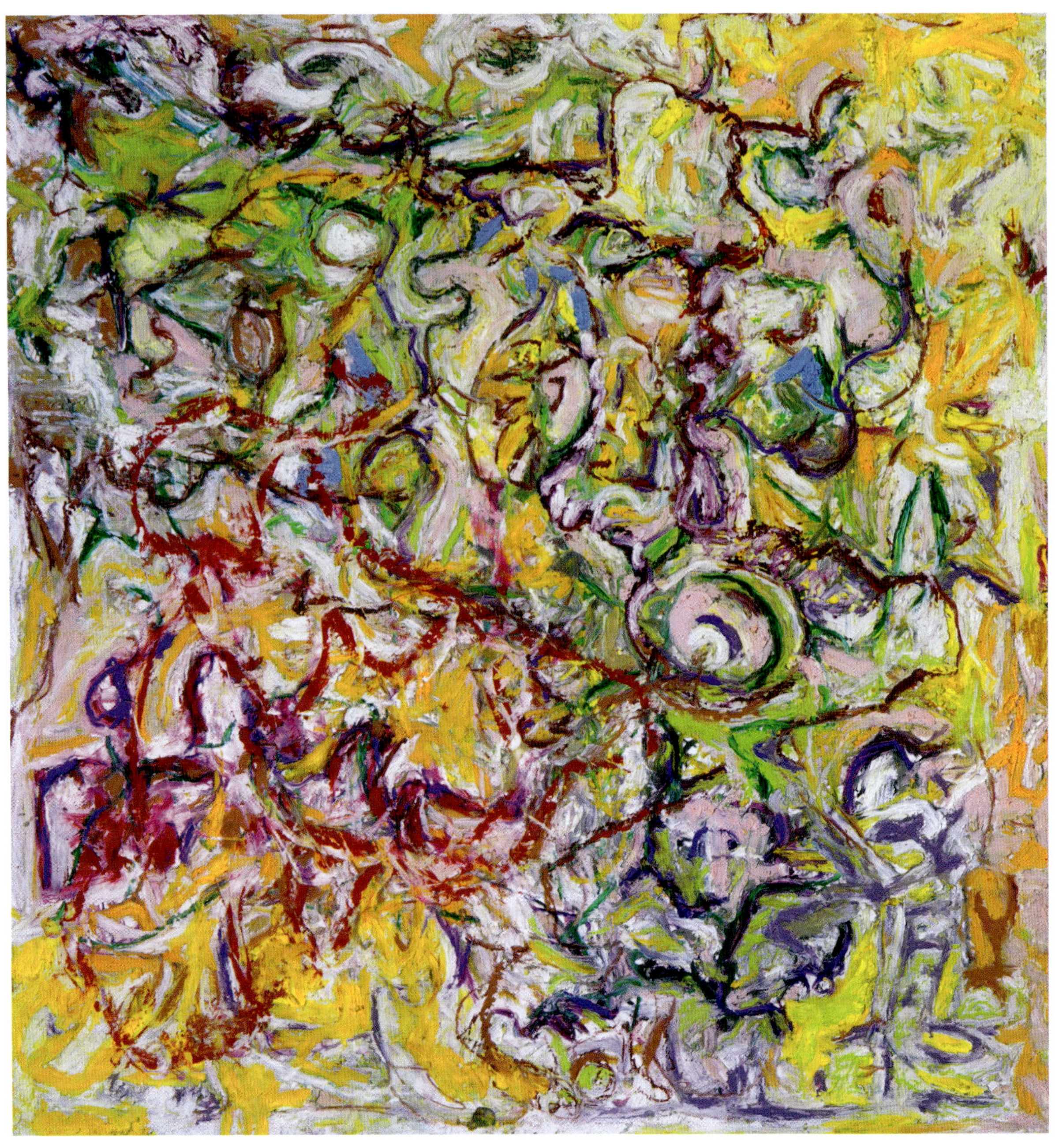

Untitled, 2006, oil on pastel board, 23 x 23½ in.

Dyrk Meyers

Class of 1977

Artist Dyrk Meyers, a Mount Vernon, Washington resident, has spent more than thirty years exploring oil pastels. When not working on his art, Meyers runs Oliver-Hammer Clothes Shop, a historic retail clothing company in Sedro-Woolly, Washington.

"The business and everyday family living consume a great deal of time," Meyers said. "I work my way, I investigate my way, and I experiment my way. It's thirty minutes here, three hours there; what's important is the excitement of doing," he said.

Meyers said his work is generally not thought out ahead of time, but created as he goes.

"I work into the surface through a process of applying color, scraping, applying color, grinding, smearing, and reapplying color. Changing, changing, changing, the image gradually develops on its own."

Recent Career Highlights:

- Work owned by numerous private collectors
- Owner and operator of Oliver-Hammer Clothes Shop, Sedro-Woolly, Washington

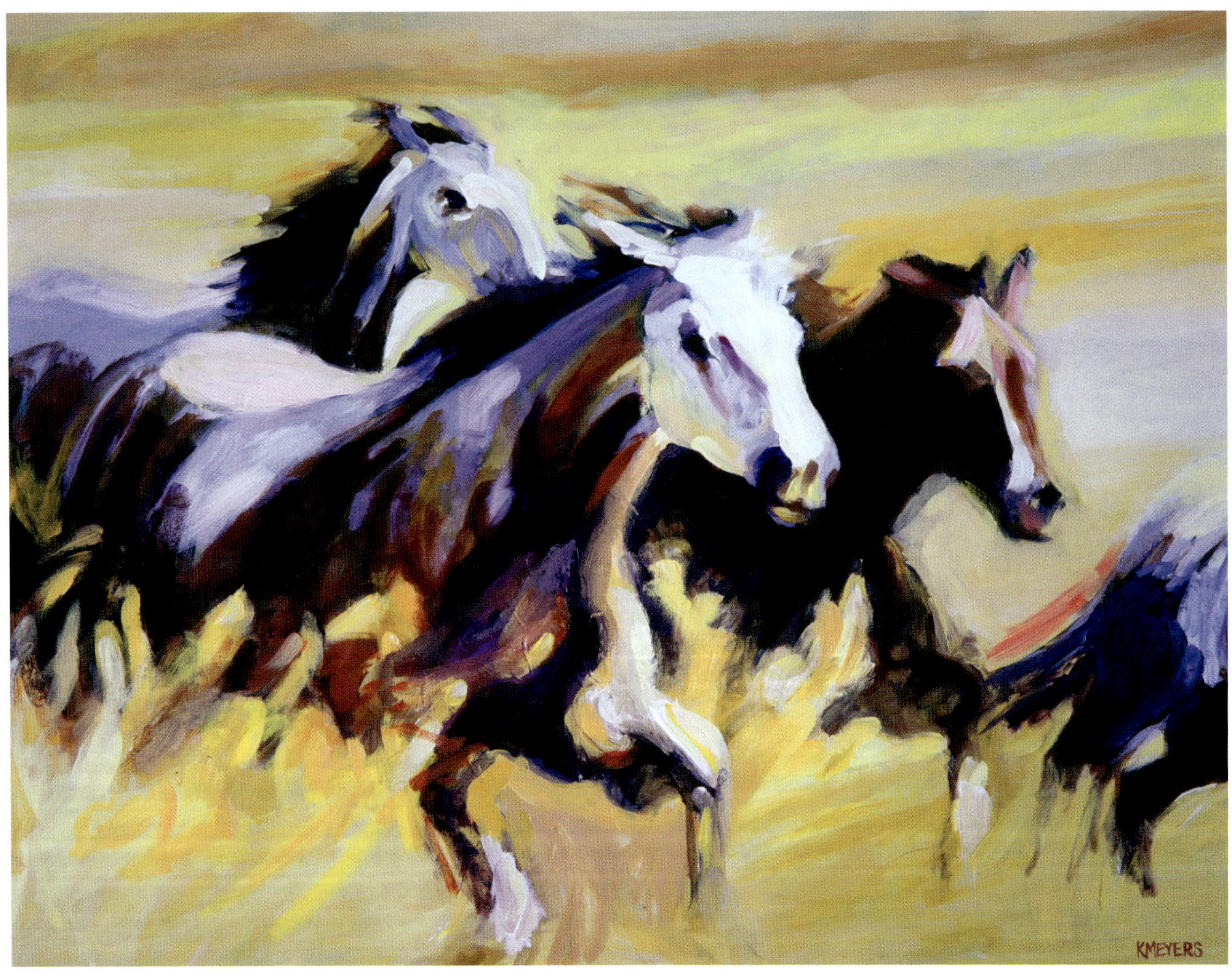

Run to Texas Creek, 2007, acrylic on canvas, 47½ x 35½ in.

Kathy Meyers

Class of 1974

Kathy Meyers's first experience with art was when she drew a horse at age five. Decades later, the Winthrop, Washington painter is still focusing most of her energies on turning the large, majestic creatures into works of art.

"Of course, my technique has improved a bit, and my horse hooves don't look like dinner plates anymore, but my enthusiasm has remained the same," Meyers said. "I am overwhelmed with the colors of the Methow Valley and the continually changing shadows of the hills and trees, not to mention the seasons and the different moods they bring."

Meyers exhibits most of her paintings at galleries in Winthrop, but she has also exhibited at many other galleries across Washington State.

Meyers belongs to several organizations, including the Society of Children's Book Writers and Illustrators, the Colored Pencil Society of America, the Pastel Society of Oregon, and the Northwest Pastel Society.

"Art and painting are passions for me and I can't think of a better way to spend a life than to wallow in color," she said.

Recent Career Highlights:

- 2006: Three-person exhibit, Winthrop Gallery, Winthrop, Washington
- 2006: Methow Arts Fest, Twisp, Washington
- 2006: *Methow Arts Magazine*, featured artist article, Twisp, Washington

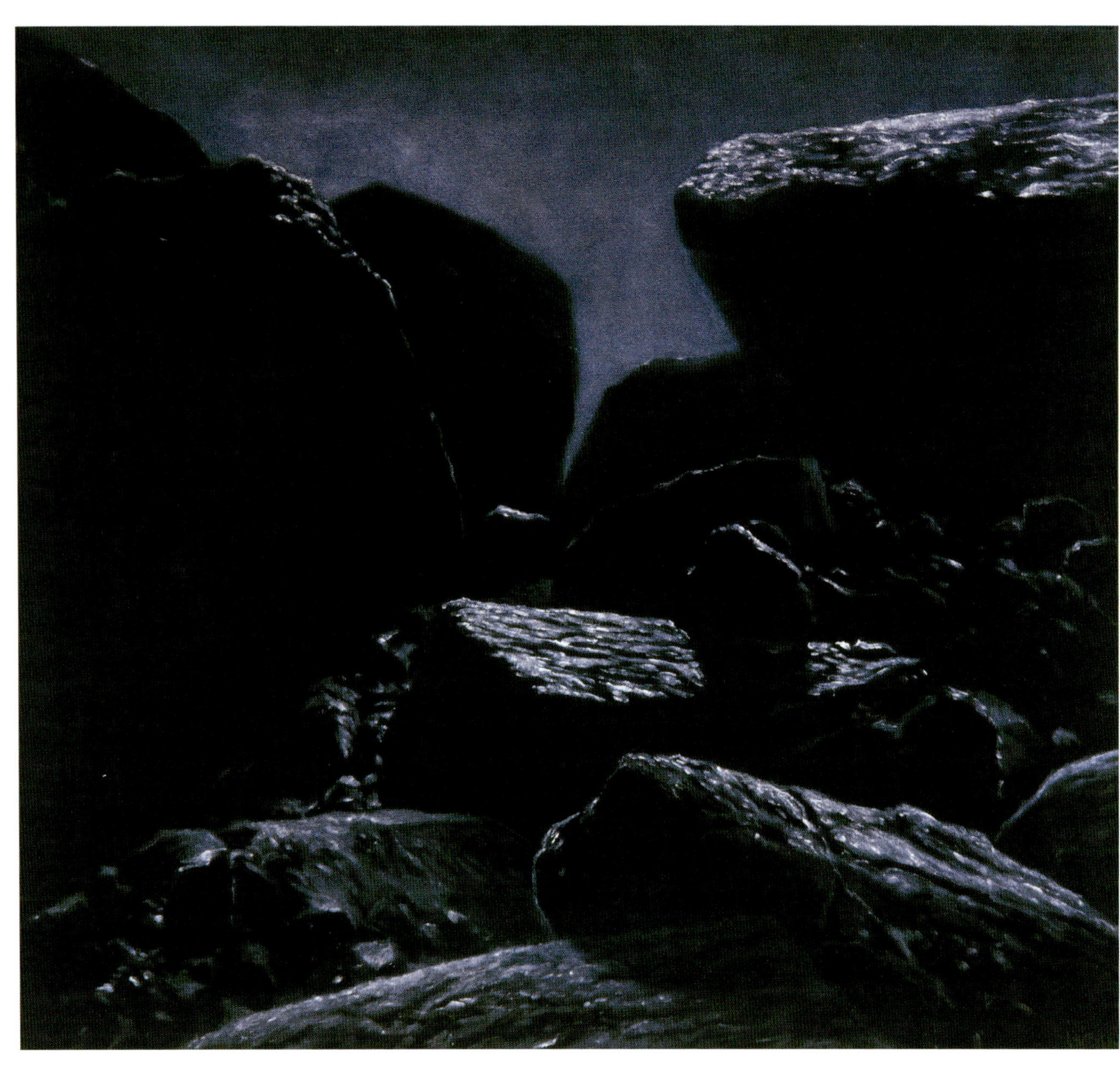

Rockslide #18, 1983, oil on black velvet, 40 x 36 in.

Alan Moen

Class of 1974

Entiat, Washington resident Alan Moen spent decades as an art educator, multi-media painter, writer, and community activist.

Most recently, Moen has worked as chairman of the Chelan County branch of the North Central Citizens for Responsible Government. In past years, he was the founding director of the Snowgrass Institute of Art in Cashmere, Washington, an instructor at City Art Works in Seattle, Washington, and an instructor at the Bellevue Art Museum in Bellevue, Washington.

Moen's had dozens of solo and group exhibits, with most of his work focusing on the natural beauty of the Pacific Northwest.

"For thirty years, my work has been a response to the mystery and power of the Northwest landscape—its logjams, rockslides, rivers, and landforms. I have often combined drawing and painting on paper with a variety of wet and dry media, including charcoal, chalk, conté crayon, pastel, watercolor, and metallic pigments," Moen said.

Along with obtaining a master's in art from Central Washington University, Moen has studied at the Cornish Institute and the School of Visual Concepts, both in Seattle, Washington.

Recent Career Highlights:

- 2003: Drawing exhibit, Confluence Gallery, Twisp, Washington
- 1997: Group exhibit, Artists of the Upper Valley, North Central Washington Museum, Wenatchee, Washington
- 1994: The Fruited Lane public art project, Cashmere, Washington

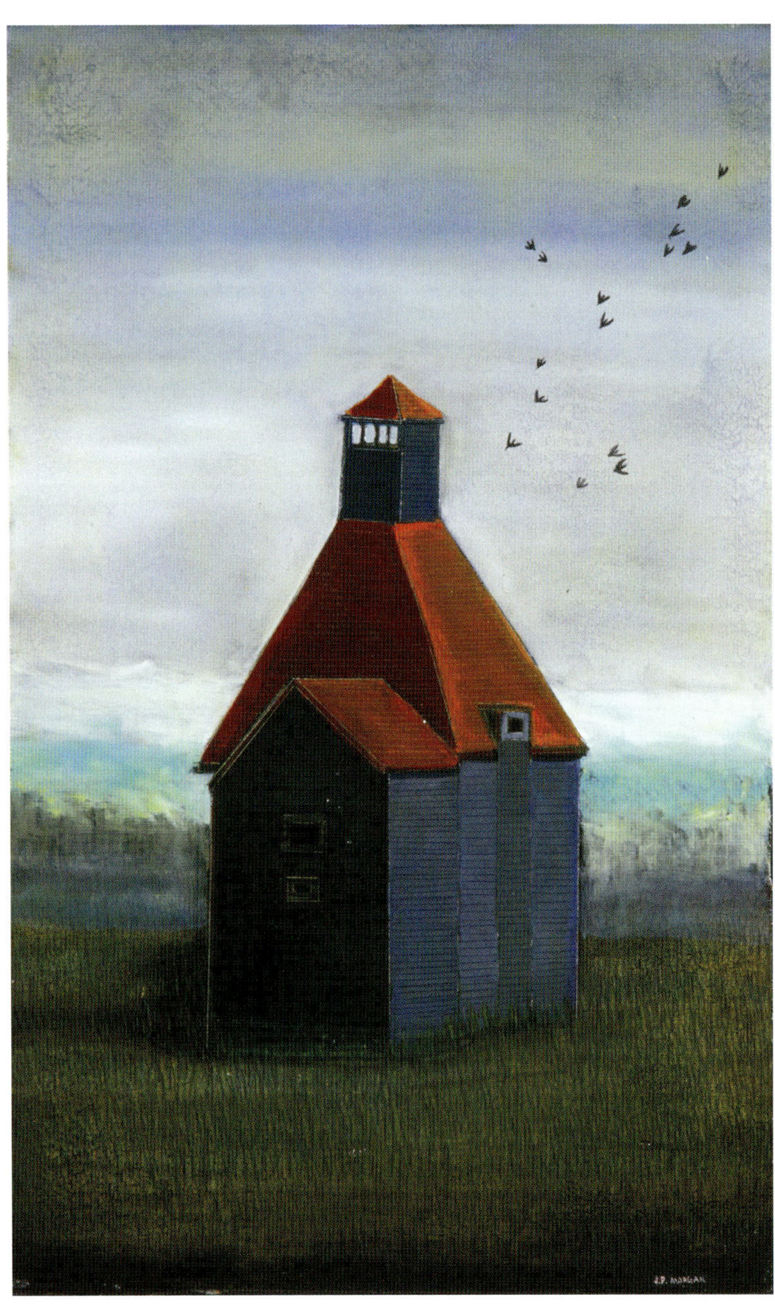

Donald's Old Hop Kiln, 2004, oil on canvas, 22¼ x 31¼ in.

John Morgan

Class of 1960 and 1968

John Morgan, a Seattle, Washington resident, began his art career as a young man growing up on a sheep ranch in central Washington. After working as an educator in both public and private schools, he eventually became a graphic artist for Boeing, where he helped animate instructional films.

Eventually his interests took him into new art forms, where he studied Japanese woodblock printmaking with internationally known artists Jun'ichro Sekino and Kiyoshi Saito. Later he learned hand-pulled lithography from fellows at the Tamarind Lithographic Institute in Albuquerque, New Mexico.

"Always active in the organizations of my chosen field, I was president of the Northwest Printmakers, and a member of the Graphics Society and Artists Equity," Morgan said.

Morgan enjoys making prints of tropical fish, frogs, and butterflies, but exotic birds, such as cranes, herons, hawks, ibis, and egrets tend to be found more frequently throughout his work.

"My mediums of choice, outside of printmaking, are watercolor, colored pencil, pen and ink, cutting, and assembling," he said.

Recent Career Highlights

- 2007: Group Christmas exhibition, East Shore Gallery, Bellevue, Washington
- 2006: Group exhibit Northwest Crafts Center, Seattle Center, Seattle, Washington
- Various pieces on exhibit at Northwest galleries, including Earthworks, Yachats, Oregon, Oceanic Arts, Newport, Oregon, and The Real Mother Goose, Portland, Oregon

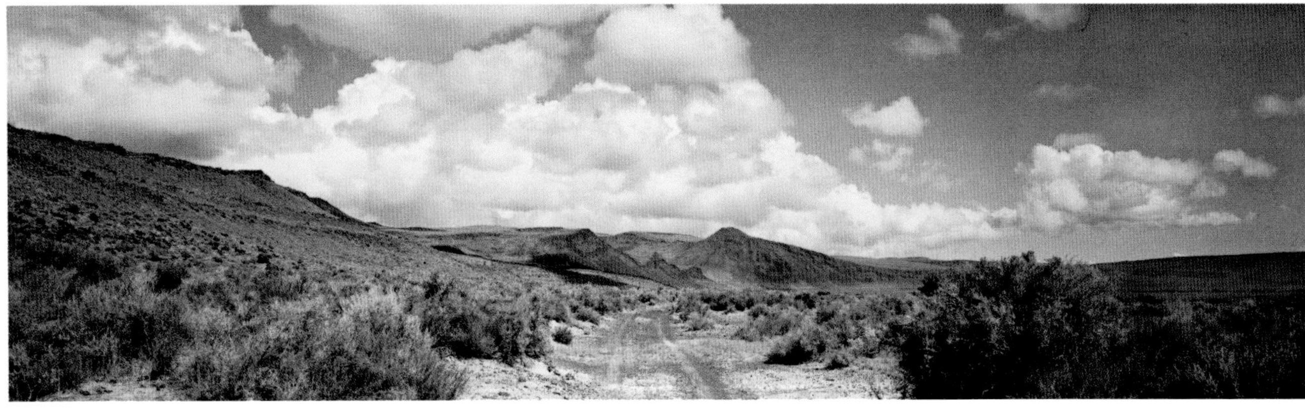

"Ranch Road: Summer Lake," 2006, digital print, 20 x 5½ in.

Kurt Norlin

Class of 1972 and 1974

Artist Kurt Norlin first became interested in panoramic photography when he looked at an old image of a Seattle, Washington fire station, where his grandfather worked. The panoramic shot gave Norlin a real sense of being there, and it was one he wanted to learn to duplicate.

"Since that time, I have constructed an occasional segmented, or joiner style of panoramic image, but it was my introduction to digital cameras, Photoshop®, and the Malheur Photographic Workshop in Oregon's high desert that really spurred my interest again," he said.

Currently, Norlin teaches photography at Linn-Benton Community College in Albany, Oregon, and exhibits his work regularly. He has participated in juried and invitational exhibits, and has also curated several others.

Most of his curatorial experience has been at the community college where he teaches, but he has also curated exhibitions at the Benton County Historical Museum in Philomath, Oregon.

Recent Career Highlights:

- 2007: Curator of Light Box 4, an international alternative photography exhibit, Linn-Benton Community College, Albany, Oregon
- 2006: Art about Agriculture, Oregon State University, Corvallis, Oregon
- 2006: Panoramic Photographs three-person exhibit, Linn-Benton Community College, Albany, Oregon

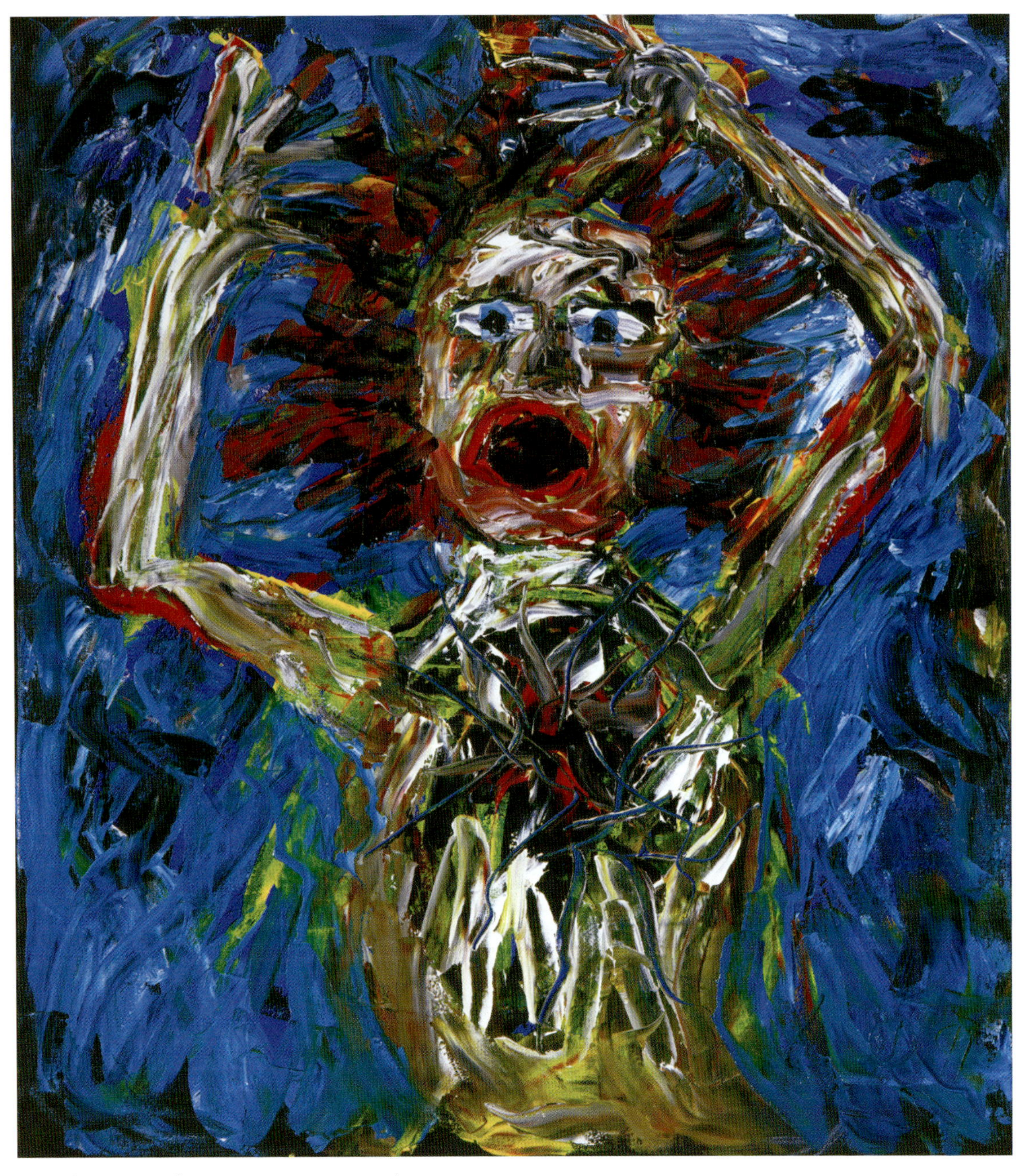

I Feel, 1991, oil on canvas, 37½ x 41½ in.

Jane Orleman

Class of 1971

Ellensburg, Washington resident Jane Orleman recently completed a new series of paintings titled "Beneath the Canopy of Heaven," which were exhibited for the first time at Central Washington University's Sarah Spurgeon Gallery in 2007. The large oil paintings, created between 2004 and 2007, are filled with goddesses and dream images that refer back to Orleman's inner psychological and spiritual state.

Prior to completing this new work, Orleman spent more than a decade focusing her skills on a series of more than 350 paintings addressing childhood trauma. The paintings eventually culminated in a book titled *Telling Secrets: An Artist's Journey through Childhood Trauma.* A $100,000 Paul Allen Foundation grant funded the book, published by the Child Welfare League of America.

"One hundred and five paintings were reproduced in full color along with my written account of that journey," Orleman said. Solo exhibitions from the series appeared in university art galleries in Washington, Montana, Wyoming, California, and Oregon, as well as at several non-profit venues.

Recent Career Highlights:

- 2007: Solo exhibit, Chase Gallery at City Hall, Spokane, Washington
- 2007: Solo exhibit, Beneath the Canopy of Heaven, Sarah Spurgeon Gallery, Central Washington University, Ellensburg, Washington
- 2005: Allied Arts of Yakima Valley 38th Annual Juried Art Show, Yakima, Washington

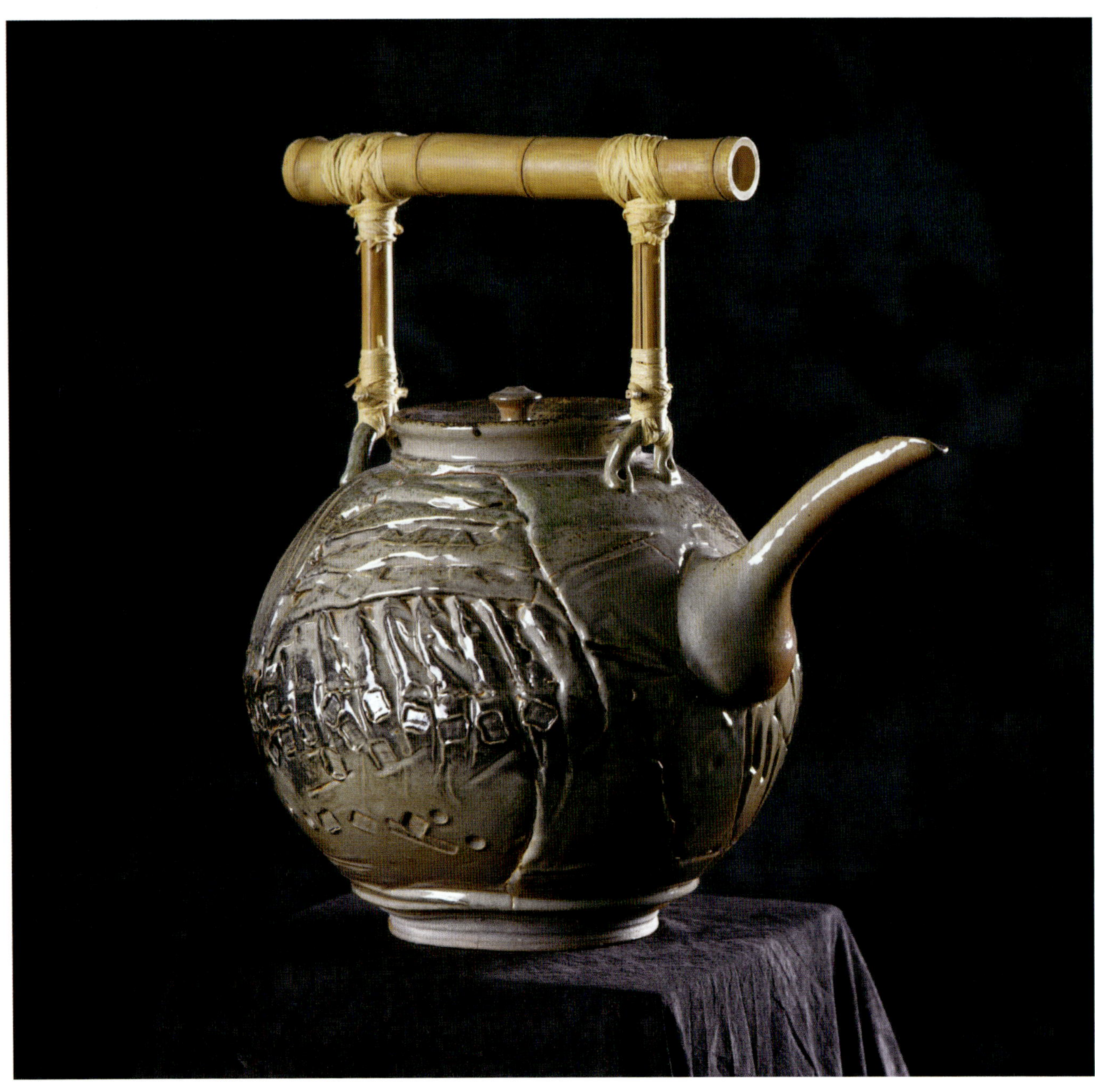

Tea Pot, 2007, ash and shino glaze, ceramic, 13 x 19 x 18½ in.

Jack Osier

Class of 1971 and 1978

Ceramicist Jack Osier, a Vancouver, Washington resident, has exhibited his work throughout the Pacific Northwest, and spent many years as an arts educator as well.

"Among the most important resources in our culture are the arts. The arts, in my case pottery, provide students with opportunity to use their imagination, to create multiple solutions to problems, and to rely on their judgment to determine when a problem is solved or a project is complete," he said.

When not teaching, Osier spends his time working with clay. "My work deals with the manipulation of clay bodies and surfaces to show the relationship and quality of traditional and non-traditional approaches to forming clay. The surfaces are enhanced with a combination of techniques, such as striking, printing, slapping, stamping, tearing, ripping, and throwing."

Recent Career Highlights:

- 2006: Group exhibition, Looking Forward, Glancing Back: Northwest Designer Craftsmen at 50, Bellevue Arts Museum, Bellevue, Washington
- 2005: Exhibition at the Contemporary Crafts Gallery, Portland, Oregon
- 2005: Exhibition at the Wenatchee Valley County Art Museum, Wenatchee, Washington

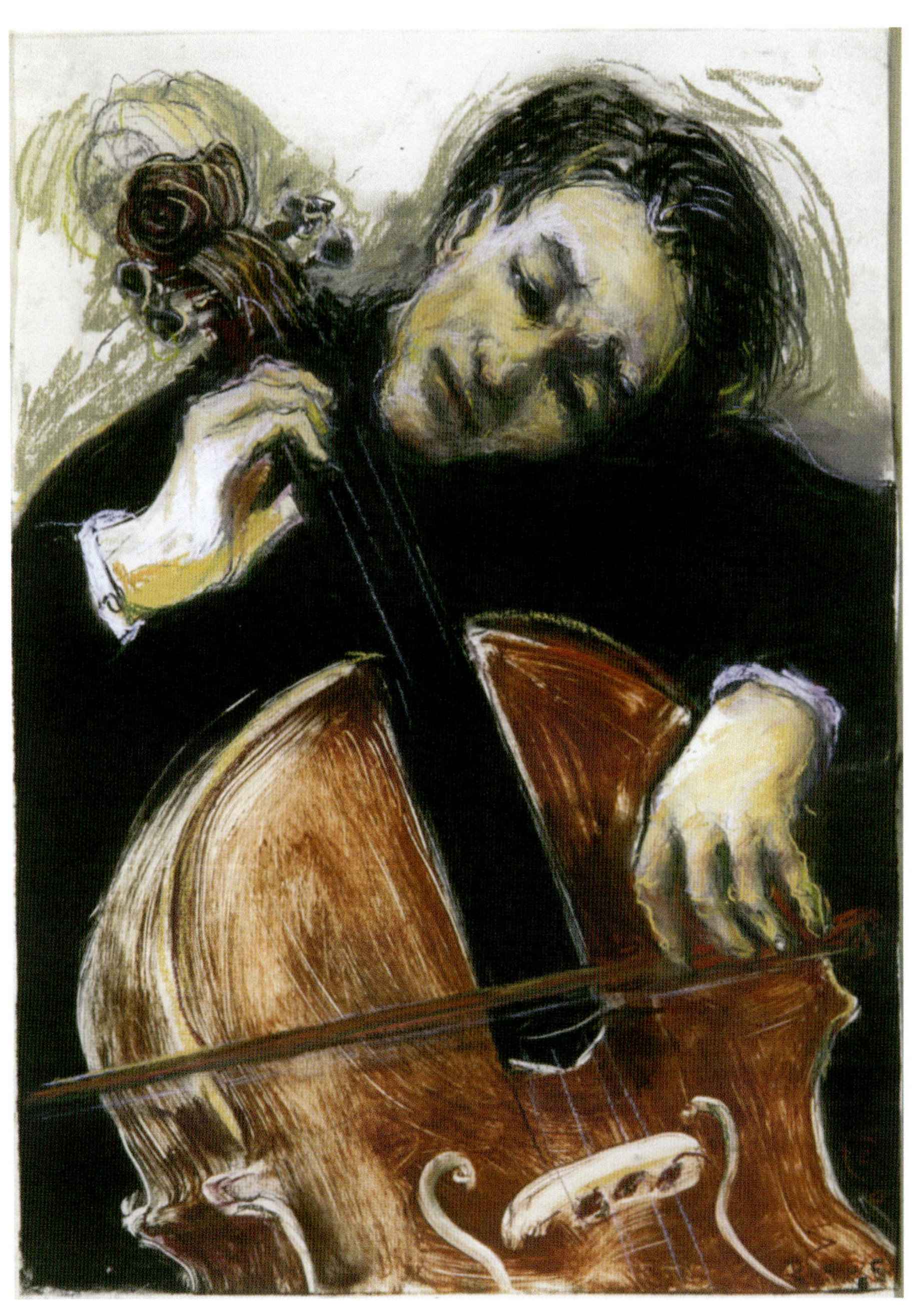

Cello Suite, 2005, monotype with pastel, 15¼ x 21 in.

Elizabeth Otto

Class of 1974 and 1984

Elizabeth Otto, a Salem, Oregon resident, has spent her life focusing on drawing, printmaking, and painting. Since 1982, she has created monotype prints that she then uses as a source of inspiration to develop the composition and content of her paintings.

"Watercolors have been my mainstay when traveling, but when I am home in my studio, the printing press and easel are the centers of my work," Otto said. "The human figure has remained the primary source of structure and meaning for my work, whether in landscape or portraiture."

Over the past forty years, Otto has lived and worked in several African countries. Her experiences there have deeply influenced her art.

"My first job as an artist was in Ethiopia, and when, in 1991, Ethiopia's military dictator was finally overthrown after seventeen years of brutal control, I spent the next two years creating fifteen large paintings and ten prints from on-site drawings that I had completed in Ethiopia before the revolution," she said.

Recent Career Highlights:

- 2006: National University of Lesotho Drama Department stage design, Roma, Lesotho, Africa
- 2006: National University of Lesotho solo exhibit portraits and watercolors, Roma, Lesotho, Africa
- 2005 and 2006: Portrait workshop instructor, Larson Gallery, Yakima, Washington

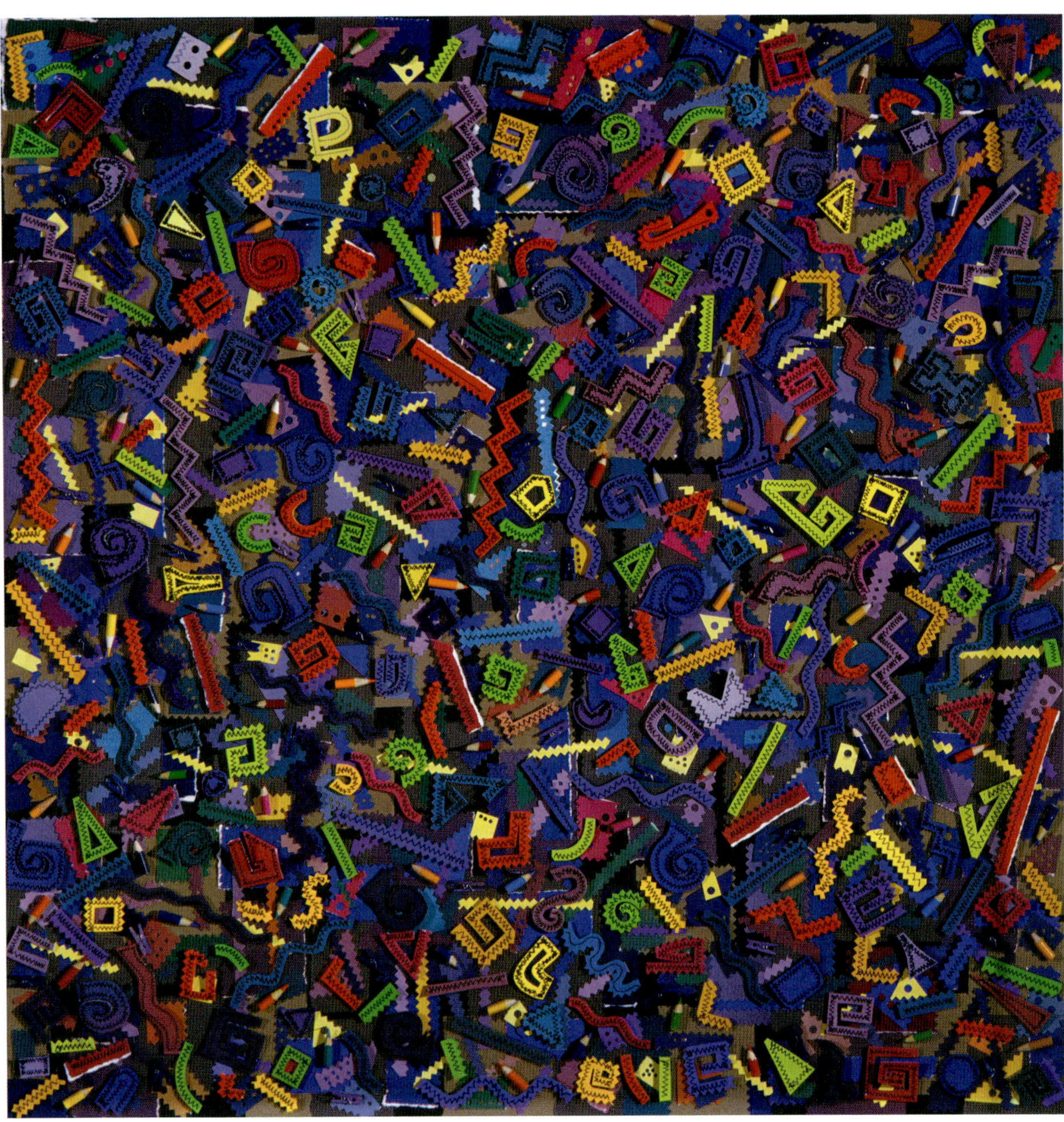

Somewhere on My Desk, 2006, mixed media, 34½ x 34½ x 1¾ in.

Robert Purser

Class of 1962

Since 1966, Robert Purser has taught art at Bellevue Community College. In between time spent in the classroom, Purser, a Bellevue, Washington resident, focuses on his artwork, which consists primarily of large sewn paper works, combined with found objects.

"In the past my work was highly analytical and geometric. For many years I was inspired by quilt patterns and did a number of thematic pieces using sewn paper and found objects," Purser said.

For several years after that, he abandoned most of his geometric works for a new style; however, recently, he has returned to some of his original methods.

"I have returned to grids, but ones with less structure," he said. "I still create sewn shapes in paper, and I attempt to merge the informality of the layered works with structure," he said. "However, using twigs, nature presents a softer structure. At this point I am between the desire to explore more color relations in the layered works and this recent direction that combines sewn paper with nature's grid."

Recent Career Highlights:

- 2006: Group exhibit, Looking Forward, Glancing Back: Northwest Designer Craftsmen at 50, Bellevue Arts Museum, Bellevue, Washington
- 2005: Kirkland Performing Arts Center exhibit, Kirkland, Washington
- 2003: 2+2=Art, the Art of Mathematics exhibit, Snohomish County Art Gallery, Everett, Washington

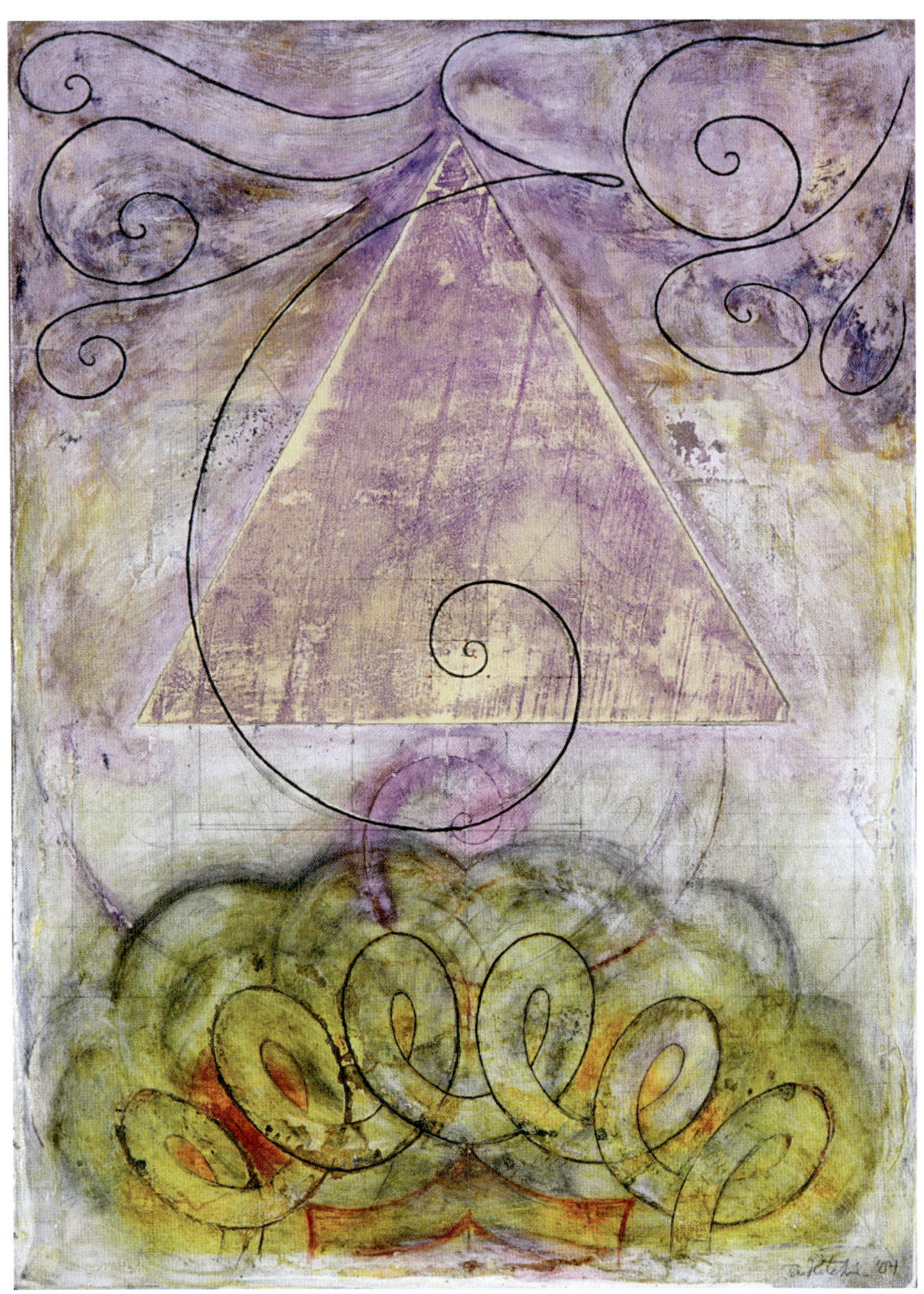

Craft with Spiral, 2005, mixed media, 12 x 16 in.

Bill Ritchie

Class of 1966

Seattle artist Bill Ritchie credits his four years spent in Ellensburg, Washington, and his childhood spent in the Yakima Valley as major influences in his present-day art.

"I brought the rural influence with me to San Jose in my graduate work," he said.

Ritchie earned a master's degree in printmaking from San Jose State University in California, a bachelor's degree in art from Central Washington University, and has displayed his work in several exhibitions.

Ritchie also creates Web-based educational programs and art education technology. Previously, from 1966 to 1985, he worked as a professor of art, traditional printmaking, and media arts, for the University of Washington. During that time, he produced videos on media arts and developed and tested prototypes of electronic texts on art studio practices.

Recent Career Highlights:

- Created an unpublished, interactive game titled Emeralda
- 2007 and 2006: Seattle Print Fair participant, Seattle, Washington
- 2005: Artist Trust Auction demonstrator of the mini press, Seattle, Washington

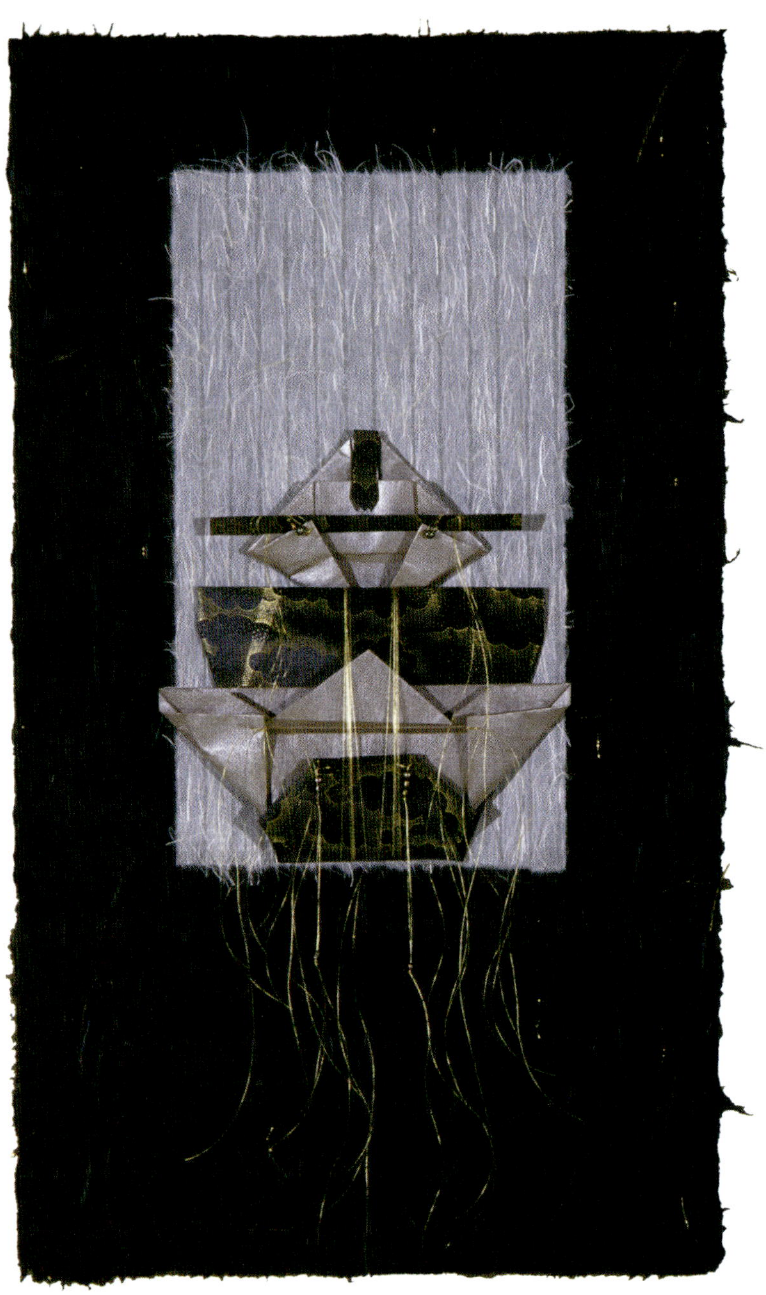

Terrigami I, 2005, mixed media, 14 x 24 in.

Terri Schaake

Class of 1971

Central Washington University graduate Terri Schaake was instrumental in starting the ArtsVan program. Over the years, she traveled with ArtsVan throughout the Yakima Valley, where she taught art at various grade schools.

"ArtsVan is still operating under the guidance of Allied Arts of Yakima Valley, in Yakima," Schaake said. "It is an educational vehicle that encourages creativity among Yakima Valley youth. I traveled, usually two times a week, to various schools here in the Yakima Valley and presented a variety of integrated art experiences during those years."

The Yakima, Washington artist's own work focuses on drawing and printmaking techniques, as well as folded paper collages that are influenced by origami.

"My works are not representational—they just happen as I fold. The papers used are all handmade, collected from many sources."

The Schaake family has stayed involved with Central Washington University over the years with the Schaake Endowment, which supports scholarships for music students and Wildcat Athletics.

Recent Career Highlights:

- 2007: Work exhibited at the Yakima Country Club, Yakima, Washington
- 2006: Installed commissioned work in Memorial Hospital, Yakima, Washington
- Frequently provides artwork to La Casa Hogar's fundraising auctions, Yakima, Washington

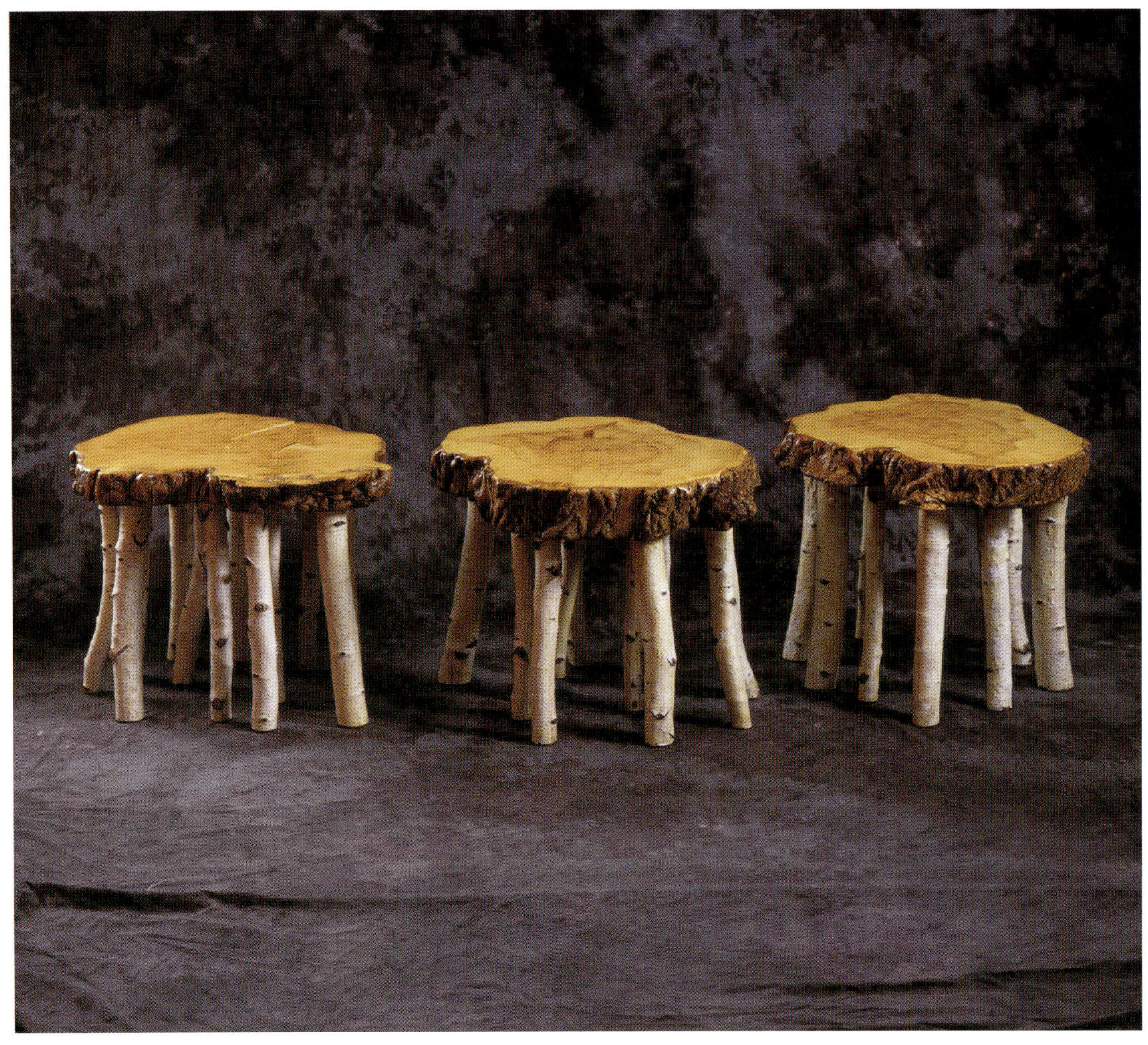

Three Tables, 2007, box elder and birch wood, 26 x 22 x 20½ in.

Chris Schambacher

Class of 1975

Ellensburg, Washington woodworker Chris Schambacher has spent his life creating detailed, organic, and ornate pieces for people's homes and public viewing.

One of his recent pieces, *Three Tables*, was completed in 2007, and is, according to Schambacher, "The legacy of two trees that grew on sites where structures now stand. The wood is cracked from age and bored by bugs, hardly suitable even for firewood. Yet these were the major qualities that drove me to transform such uncompromising material into art furniture."

One of his most recognizable pieces, the *Elephant Desk*, can be found in Central Washington University's Science Building on the second floor. The piece was published in a 1981 *Time Life Magazine* book on advanced woodworking.

Schambacher's work has been added to private collections across the Northwest. One of his biggest projects, a home in Ellensburg known as the *Love Shack*, started out a crooked, sinking structure which he transformed into a piece of livable art.

"It combines Roman, Middle Eastern, Asian, and French Deco touches, along with American craftsman architectural styles. Surprise touches reflecting artistry and craftsmanship are found throughout the house."

Recent Career Highlights:

- 2006: Clymer Museum of Art donation of handmade wooden portable bar, Ellensburg, Washington
- 2004: *Deco Moderne* entertainment center and bookcases built for private buyer
- 1998: *Hot Tub World*, large outdoor garden architecture for private buyer

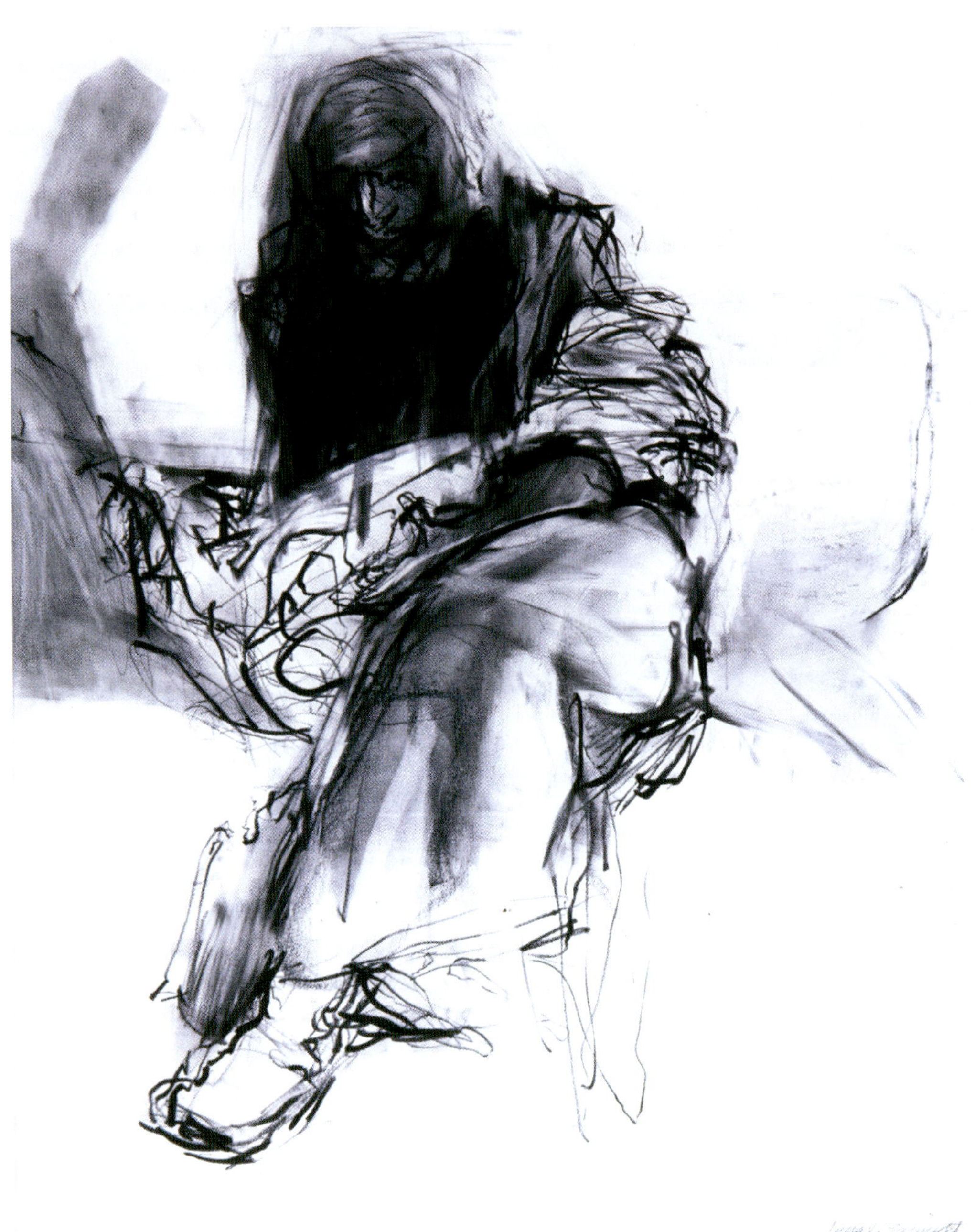

Dark Figure, 2007, graphite on paper, 13½ x 16½ in.

Teresa Tempero Schmidt

Class of 1969 and 1971

Art alumna Teresa Tempero Schmidt, a Manhattan, Kansas professor of art, recently noted that despite her relocation to the Midwest, much of her graphite drawings are still inspired by her experiences while growing up in the Northwest.

"Originally from the Pacific Northwest, I am visually influenced by light from the ocean and the movement of clouded mountains. My work is about spirituality, spatial movement, light, and transparency," she said.

Since 2002, Schmidt has taught drawing at Kansas State University. In 1998, she took several KSU students to Scotland and England for a study abroad trip, and in 1997, Schmidt taught at the Norwich School of Art & Design in Norwich, England.

She is affiliated with several galleries, including Seattle's Catherine Person Gallery and Modern Arts Midwest in Lincoln, Nebraska, and displays her work in solo and group exhibits multiple times per year.

Recent Career Highlights:

- 2006: Solo exhibit, Black & White, Chapman Gallery, Manhattan, Kansas
- 2006: Second Annual Small Works Exhibition group exhibit, Wish List, Modern Arts Midwest, Lincoln, Nebraska
- 2005: University Small Research Grant, Kansas State University, Arts & Sciences, Manhattan, Kansas

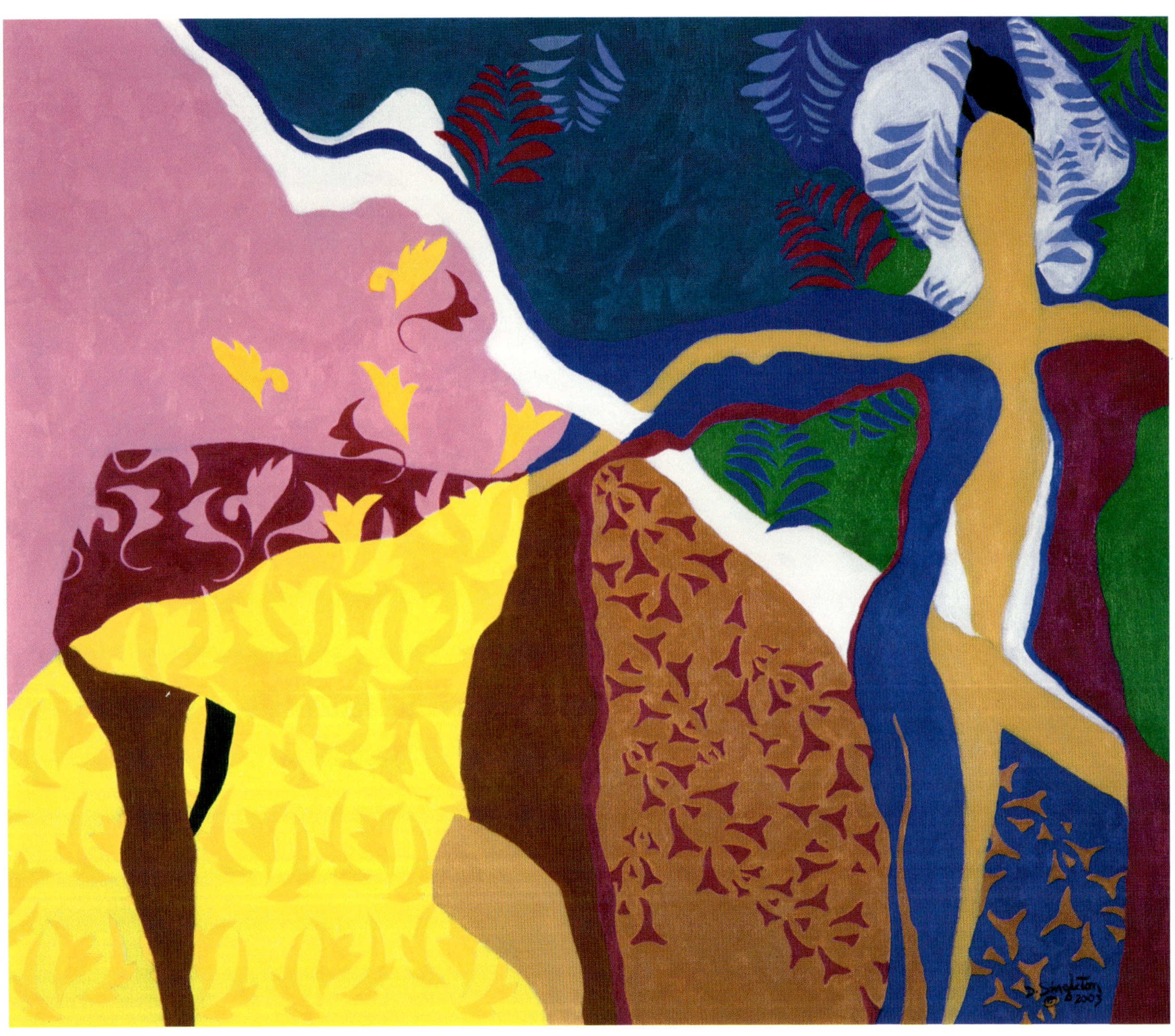

Composition for Pan Pipe and Flute, 2003, oil on canvas, 35½ x 29¼ in.

Don Singleton

Class of 1963

Prior to attending Central Washington University, painter Don Singleton, an Anacortes, Washington resident, worked as a photographer in the U.S. Air Force from 1955 to 1959. In 1963 he graduated with his bachelor of arts from CWU, and in 1967, he earned a master of arts in painting from the University of Oregon.

Recently, Singleton has focused on integrating other art forms, including music, into his paintings. Examples of this include, "Composition for Pan Pipe and Flute," "Summertime, Miles D.," and "The Four Blues Sonnet."

"These paintings are part of a larger investigation into the connections that painting can make with other art forms," Singleton said.

Singleton's past exhibits have been primarily in Washington State, in cities including Pasco, Richland, Langley, Seattle, Edmonds, and Bellevue.

Recent Career Highlights

- 2003-2006: Public exhibitions at Olson Gallery, Langley, Washington
- 1998: Esvelt Gallery, Columbia Basin College, Pasco, Washington
- 1988-1992: Chochokum Arts Festival participant, Langley, Washington

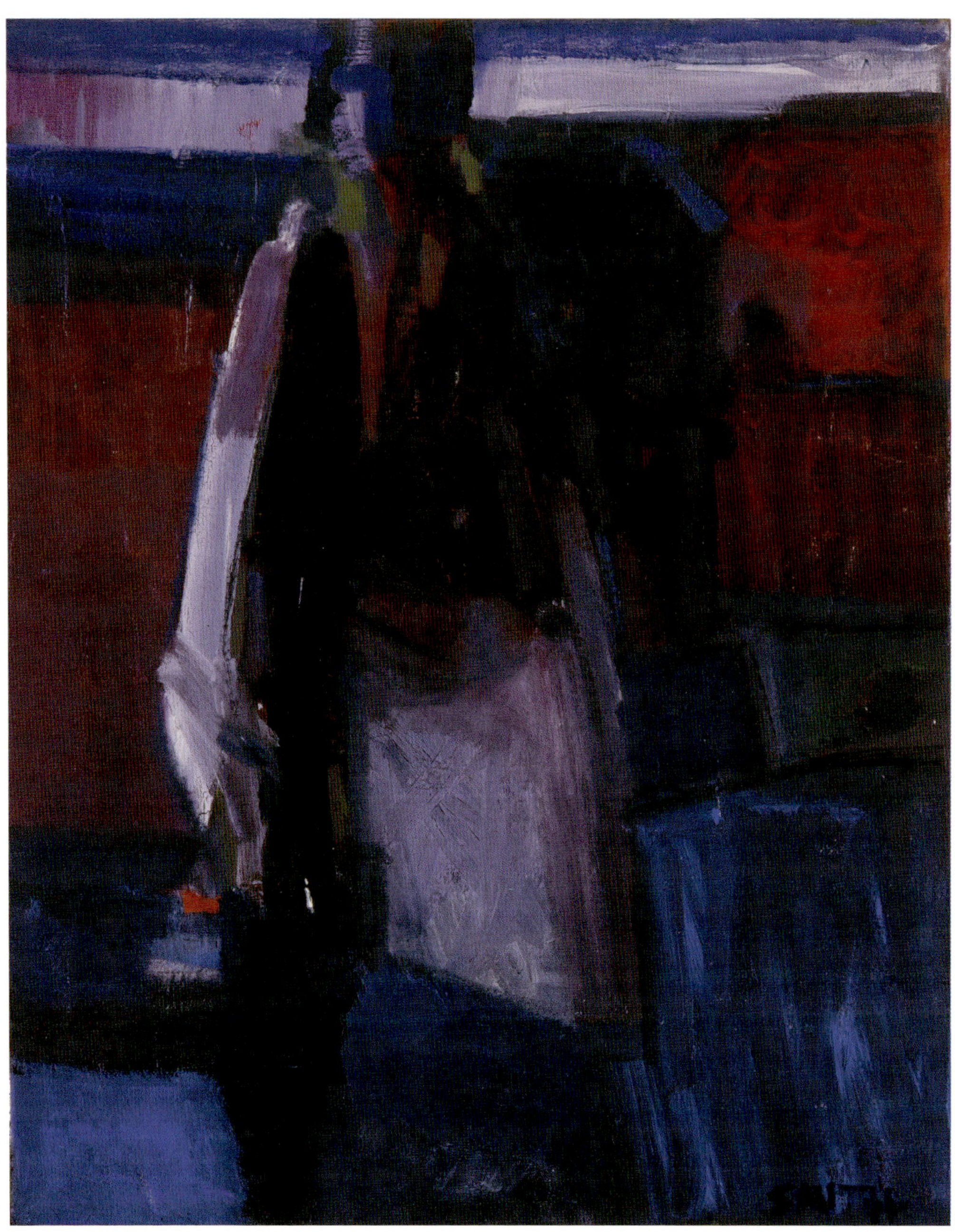

Presence, 1968, oil on canvas, 34½ x 42¼ in.

Charles Smith

Class of 1956

Yakima, Washington painter Charles Smith spent most of his adult life working as an art educator, retiring from the profession in 1993. He now spends his days as a full-time painter at his home studio.

His teaching experience spanned more than thirty years. He worked for the Auburn Public School District in Auburn, Washington, from 1958 to 1959, and then moved to Wapato, Washington, where he taught from 1960 to 1993. Each summer, from 1966 to 1977, he taught art at the University of Saskatchewan in Saskatoon, Saskatchewan, Canada.

Recent Career Highlights:

- 2008: Solo exhibit, Oak Hollow Gallery, Yakima, Washington
- 2007: Solo exhibit, Simon Edwards Gallery, Yakima, Washington
- 2006: Central Washington Artists Exhibition, Larson Gallery, Yakima, Washington

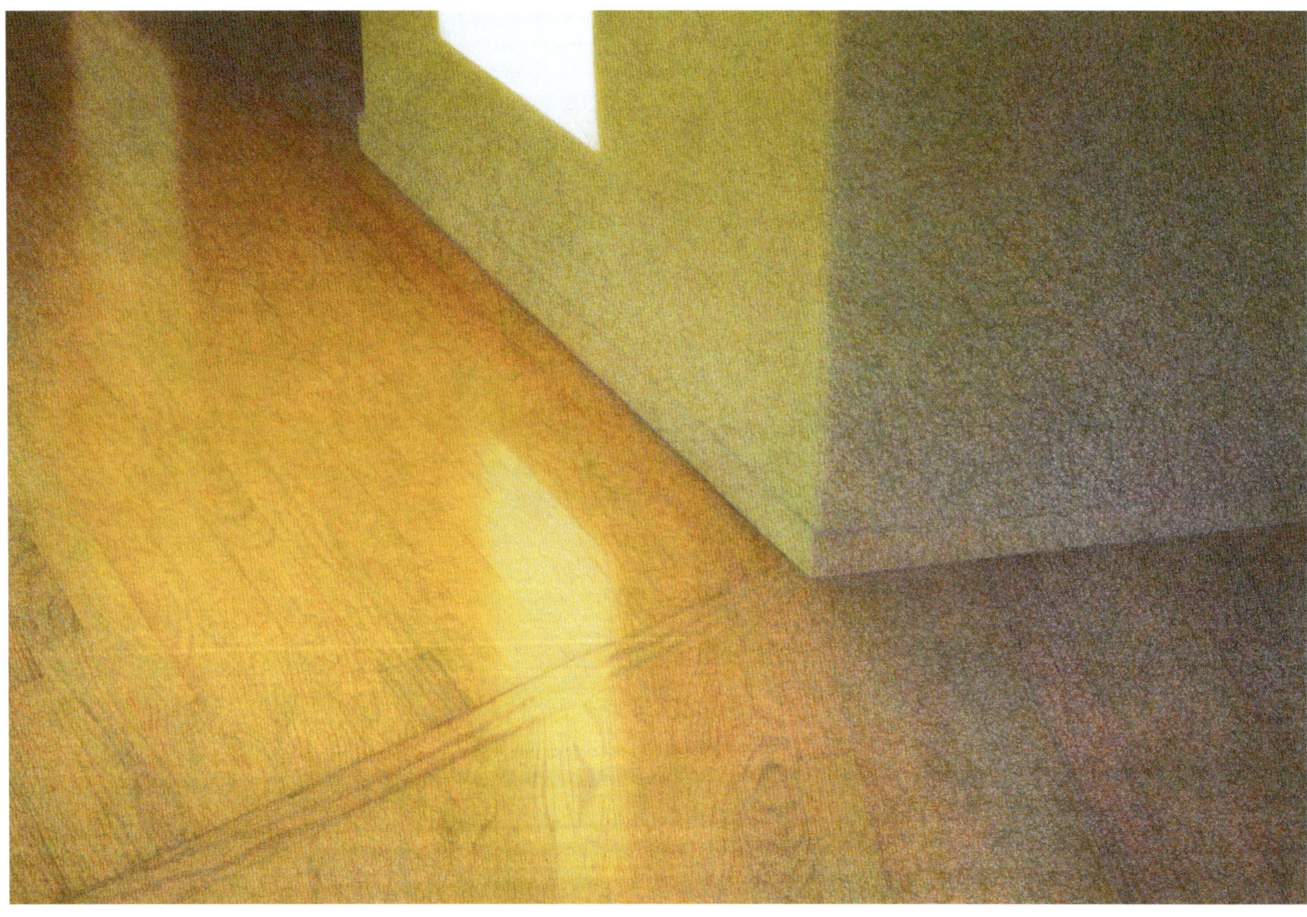

Light Filled Passage, 2005, colored pencil, 27¾ x 18½ in.

Constance Speth

Class of 1955 and 1964

Colored pencil artist Constance Speth has mastered the art of capturing light through her detailed, intimate drawings.

The Ellensburg, Washington artist has shown at many galleries across the Pacific Northwest, as well as nationally. Her works are, "a record of the passage of sunlight and shadow through the interior space of my house," Speth explained. "I typically choose a close, below eye-level view to suggest the intimate relationship between viewer and interior environment."

Often her pieces are quite large and highly detailed, with an almost photographic quality. "The simple architectural shapes in these works can be appreciated across large public spaces while the dense scumbled layering of Prismacolor pencil lines invites the viewer to take a closer look."

Speth earned a bachelor's in education at Central Washington University in 1955 and returned to CWU a few years later for a master's in education. She also obtained a master of fine arts from the University of Idaho.

She began teaching art at CWU in 1964 and retired in 1995. Her last five years at Central were spent as chair of the Department of Art.

Recent Career Highlights:

- 2007: Excellence in Drawing Award, 52nd Annual Central Washington Artists' Exhibition, Larson Gallery, Yakima, Washington
- 2006: Colored Pencil Society of America International Show, Albuquerque, New Mexico
- 2005: Solo exhibit at Gallery One Visual Arts Center, Ellensburg, Washington

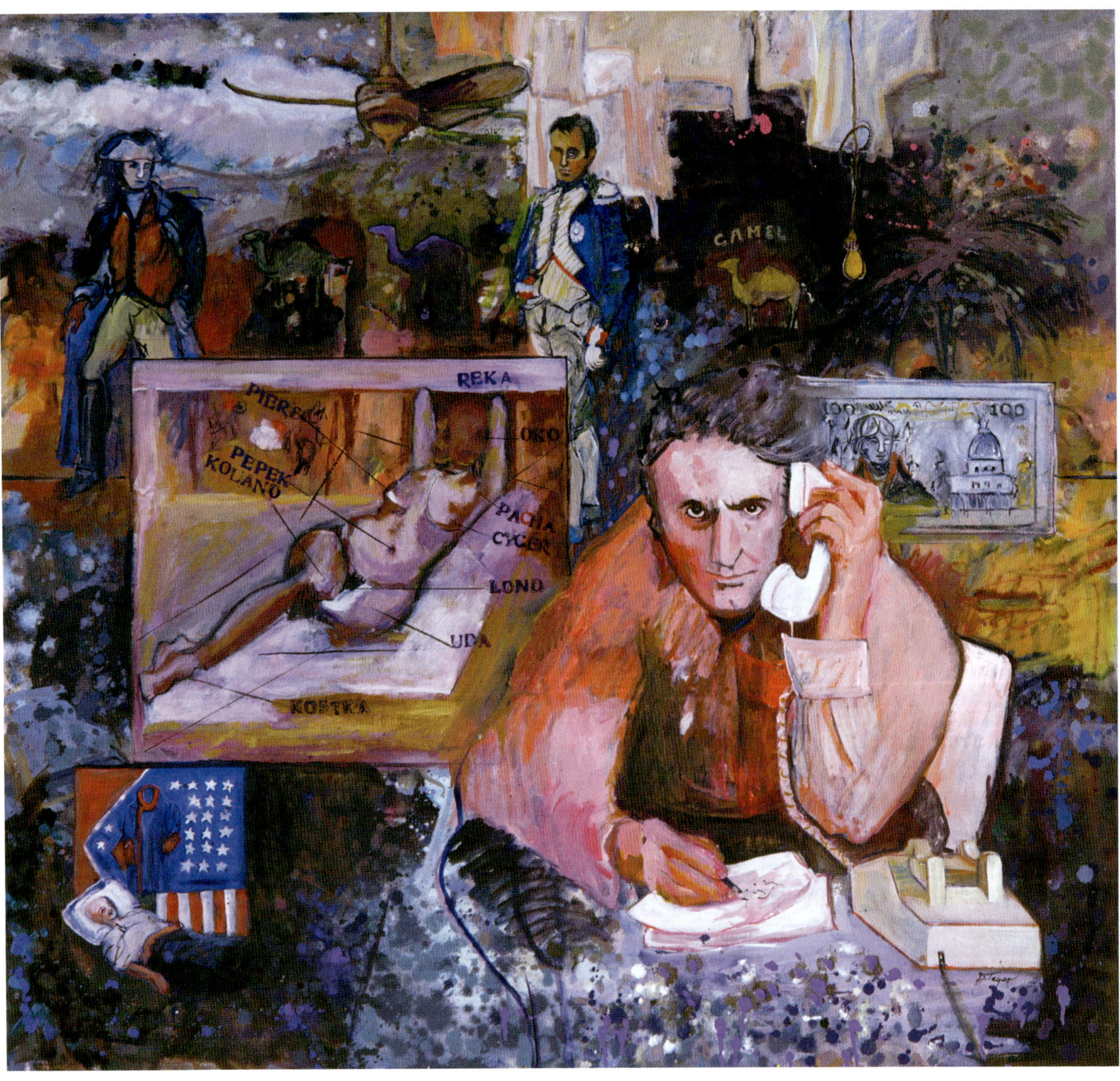

Larry Rivers, n.d., Yakima Valley Community College Larson Gallery collection, $46\frac{5}{8}$ x $42\frac{3}{4}$ in.

Delma Tayer

Class of 1962 and 1970

Delma Tayer has dedicated her life to the central Washington arts community. Her works, primarily oil paintings and pottery, have been shown throughout the region, and her expertise is often sought after.

From 1987 to 1993, she was a trustee for the Washington Commission for the Humanities. During those years, she was also a member of Ellensburg, Washington's Laughing Horse Arts Foundation. In the early 1990s, she served as president of the Washington Commission for the Humanities, now known as Humanities Washington. She also served as Dean of Arts and Sciences for Yakima Valley Community College from 1983 to 1989, as well as supervisor of Yakima's Larson Gallery.

"The arts give meaning to my life. I agree with the existentialists that it is up to the individual to attribute meaning to his or her life. I confess that for most of mine, the arts and humanities have provided my reason for being," Tayer said.

Presently, she spends most of her time working in her home studio in Selah, Washington, where she focuses on painting and pottery. "I don't just do art," she said. "I spend as much time studying the arts as I do practicing them."

Recent Career Highlights:

- 2007: 40th Annual Juried Art Exhibit, Allied Arts of Yakima Valley, Yakima, Washington
- 2001: Humanities Washington Award winner
- 2000: Larson Gallery's 2000 Woman of the Year, Yakima, Washington

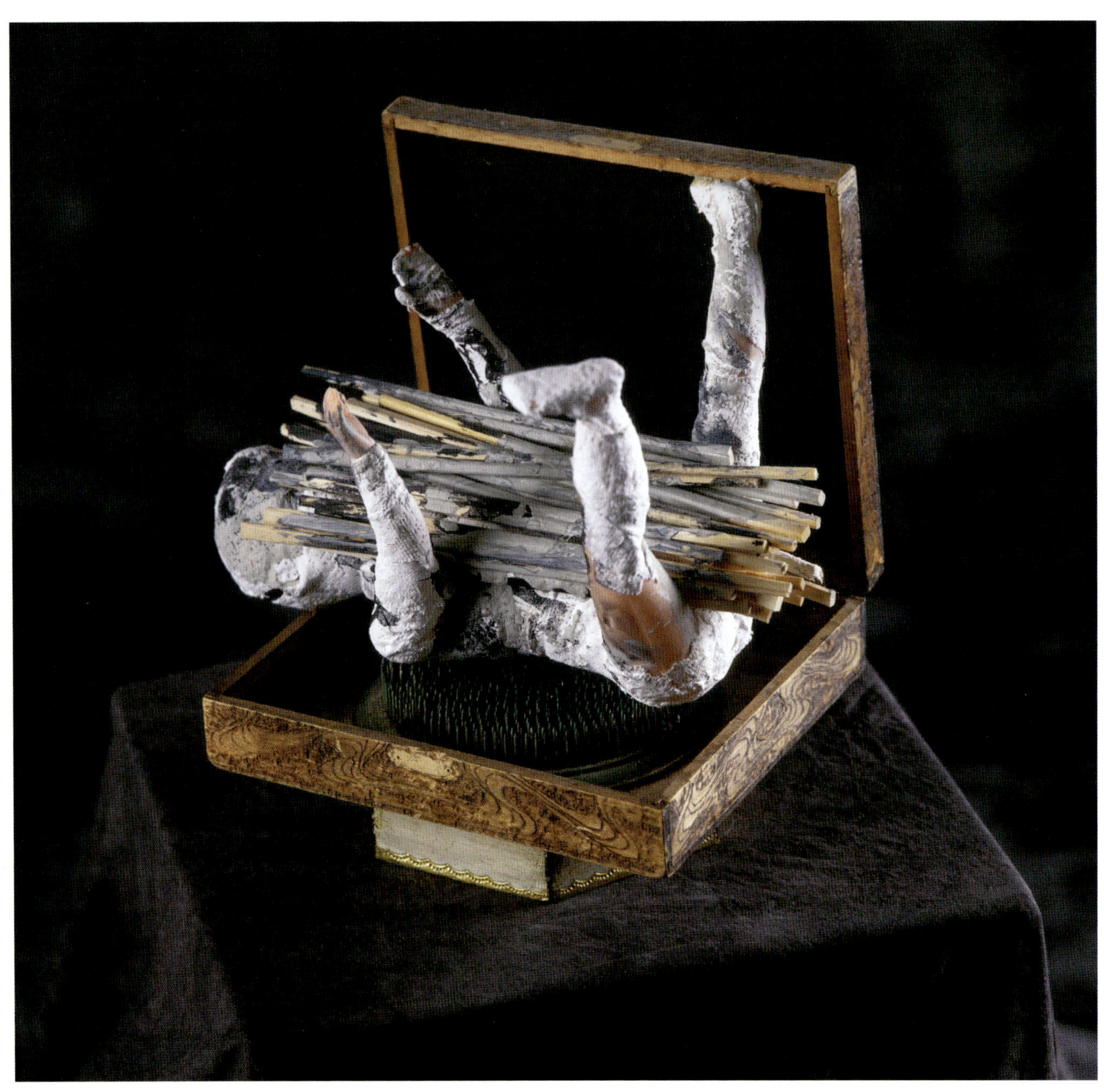

Erotic Chopstick Holder, 2004, mixed media construction, $7\frac{1}{4}$ x 11 x 10 in.

Matt Timo

Class of 1979

Seattle, Washington artist Matt Timo says what inspires him most in art is the human figure—something that keeps viewers of his artwork, as well as himself as an artist, intrigued.

"The image of an indistinct human figure has proven the most compelling for me. This figure can suggest a multitude of moods through its position in the picture plane or by its captured movement," Timo said. "By remaining faceless, it becomes a vehicle for the viewer to superimpose his or her own inquiry."

Timo, a Central Washington University master of arts in drawing and painting graduate, primarily exhibits his artwork in Seattle and in other Northwest cities. His artwork has also appeared in Finland, including exhibits at the Lönnström Art Museum and the Hagelstam Galleria.

Timo incorporates several other mediums into his paintings and drawings, including molded paper and collage, which enables him to "take challenging risks in combining elements and in creating a three-dimensional sense."

"It is important to keep risking the possible destruction of the piece by trying new approaches as I work," he said.

Recent Career Highlights:

- 2006: Wu Residence Exhibition, Lake Forest Park, Washington
- 2005: Nordic Heritage Museum, Nordic Northwest Artist Exhibition, Seattle, Washington
- 2004 and 2005: Finlandia Music & Art Festival, Freeman Gallery, Northwest College of Art, Poulsbo, Washington

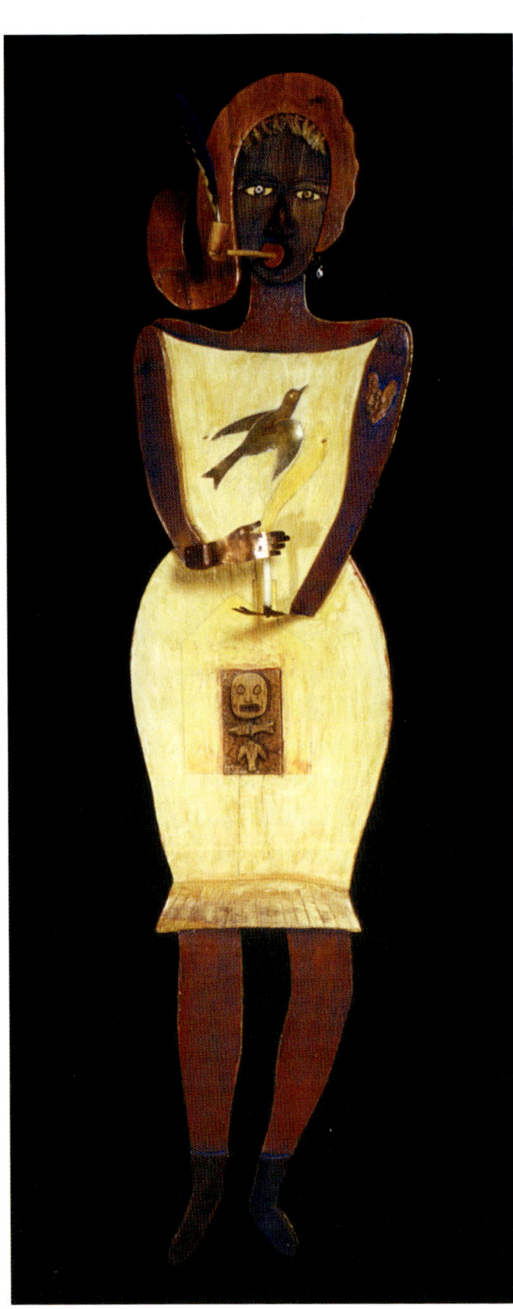

Looking for a Light, 2005, collection of Doug and Irene Baker, Seattle, Washington, mixed media, 16 x 9 x 70 in.

Merrily Tompkins
Class of 1979

Jewelry maker Merrily Tompkins grew up around other artists. Her older brother, Donald Tompkins, also a metalsmith, had a lot of influence on her as a young adult and as an artist.

"I grew up adoring Don and watching him work," she said. "My art and my life have been entwined for as long as I can remember. Making art helps me make sense of and deal with the scary and exhilarating prospect of being alive and human."

Tompkins, an Ellensburg, Washington resident, has experienced a successful career, with exhibits throughout the Northwest and in other parts of the United States. Her work can be found in several permanent public collections, including the Museum of Fine Arts in Houston, Texas, the Tacoma Art Museum in Tacoma, Washington, and the Seattle Art Museum's Anne Gerber Collection in Seattle, Washington.

Tompkins has also been featured in multiple publications, and most recently appeared in *Metalsmith* magazine's "Over Yonder," by Ben Mitchell.

Recent Career Highlights:
- 2007: Signs of Life 2007, Facèré Jewelry Art Gallery, Seattle, Washington
- 2006: Challenging the Chatelaine, Museum of Art and Design, Helsinki, Finland
- 1999: Solo exhibit, Fire in the Hole, Esther Claypool Gallery, Seattle, Washington

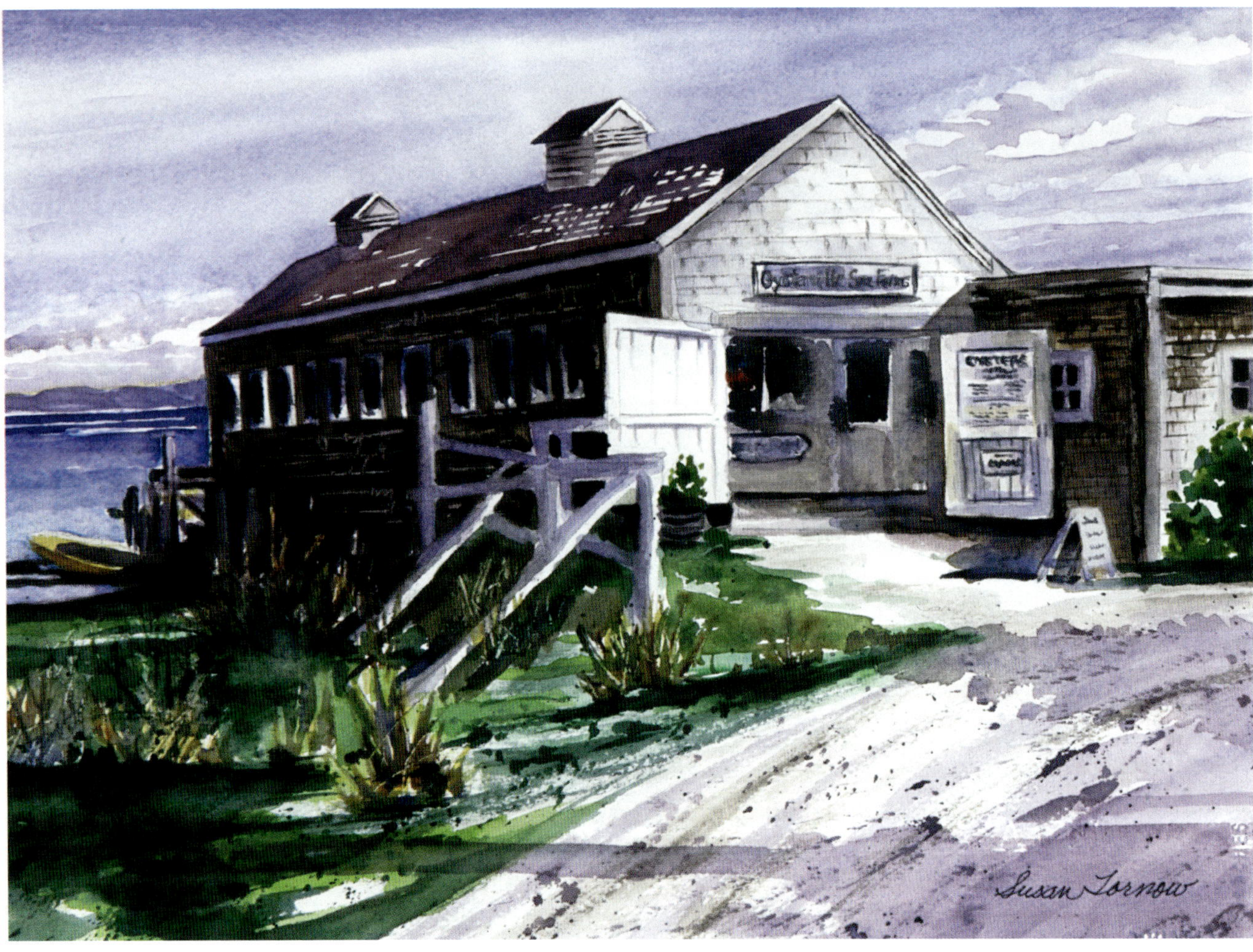

Oysterville Sea Farms, 2006, watercolor, 14½ x 10¼ in.

Susan Tornow

Class of 1971

Camas, Washington artist Susan Tornow focuses her career on transparent watercolor work. She shows and sells her watercolors with the Southwest Washington Watercolor Society, of which she is an active member.

Locally, she has exhibited in several community shows at the Camas Public Library Gallery.

"My cats and family members have become a source of inspiration for paintings as well as the landscapes of Washington State," Tornow said. "I seek self-fulfillment through art and hope to leave the joy of art with others."

In the early 1970s, Tornow taught elementary art and received her provisional teaching certificate for grades K-12 in 1976. She also volunteers, and in 2006, donated an original watercolor piece to benefit the YWCA in Clark County, Washington.

Recent Career Highlights:

- 2007: 25th Annual Art about Agriculture touring exhibit, Oregon State University, Corvallis, Oregon
- 2007: 28th Annual Southwest Washington Watercolor Society Fall Exhibit, Works in Water, Vancouver, Washington
- 2006: 27th Annual South Southwest Washington Watercolor Society Spring Exhibit, Works in Water, Vancouver, Washington

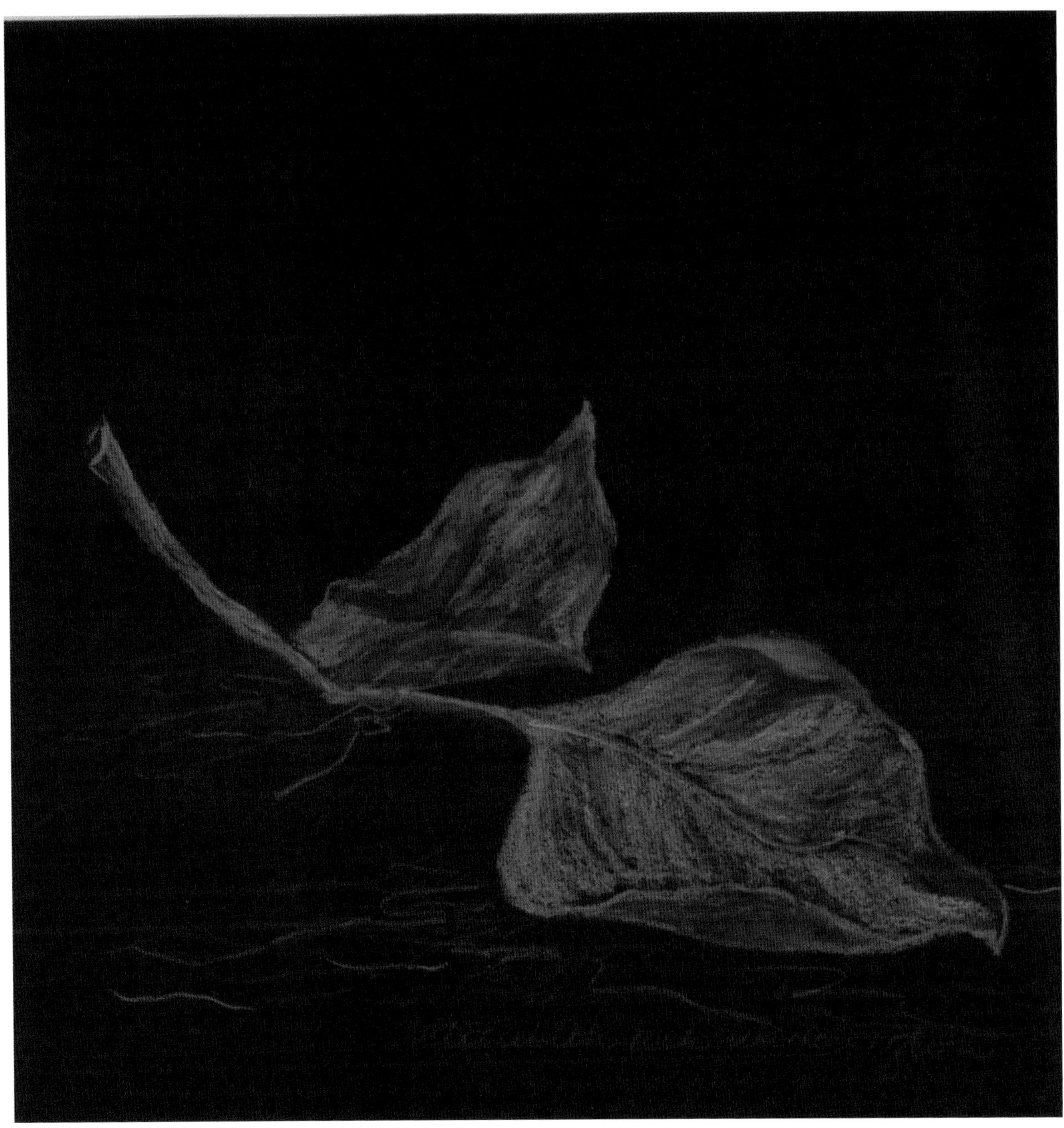

Fallen Leaves, 2005, colored pencil and pastel, 6½ x 6½ in.

Elizabeth Rock-Waddington

Class of 1976

Billings, Montana artist and librarian Elizabeth Rock-Waddington spends most of her time working in the mediums of fiber arts, watercolors, and digital photography. Since 2000, she has also worked as an adjunct professor at Montana State University in Bozeman, where she teaches online instruction for a library media program.

Montana's topography is the primary inspiration for her artwork. "The borrowed views of Montana's vast landscapes, as well as everyday surroundings, provide core images for mixed media pieces," Rock-Waddington said. "The view begins with a photo and continues past the hard edge of the print with watercolor scumbling."

Rock-Waddington spent one year, in 2001, as the chair for the Montana Art Interscholastic group, which consisted of 350 high school students who attended an overnight art retreat. From 1998 to 2006, she was also the Art Club Advisor for Billings West High School.

Recent Career Highlights:

- 2007: Yellowstone Art Auction, Yellowstone Art Museum, Billings, Montana
- 2006: Small Works Auction, Yellowstone Art Museum, Billings, Montana
- 2006: Art between Friends, Bill McIntosh Gallery, Billings, Montana

112

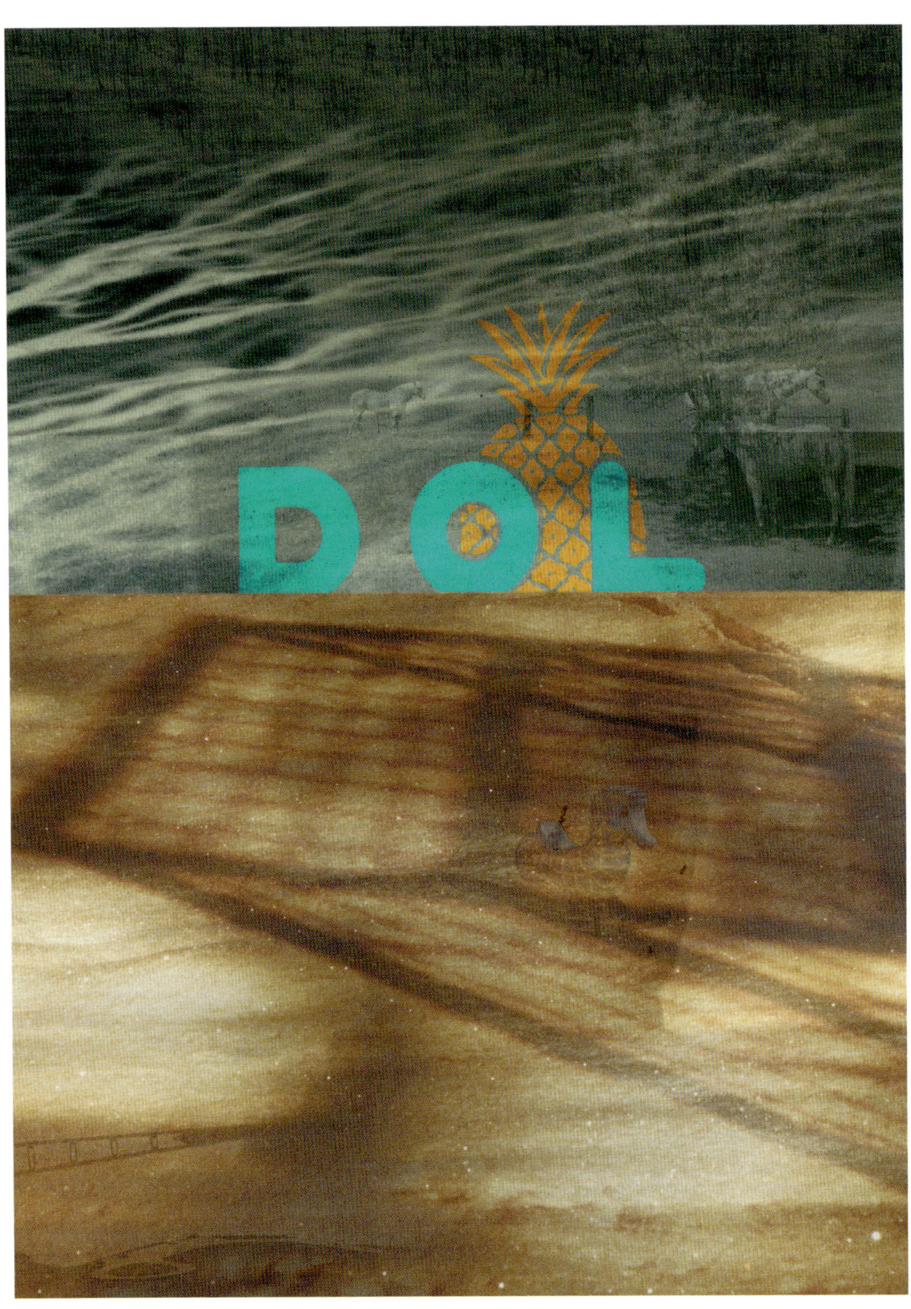

Trellis, 2007, digital inkjet print, 13¾ x 18¾ in.

Richard Warren

Class of 1970

Ellensburg, Washington graphic designer Richard Warren has owned his own design firm since 1995, specializing in commercial art, such as graphics, maps, and medical and technical illustrations made primarily for the legal field.

"In my personal work I use digital photographs with a focus on the iconic rather than the pictorial aspects of images. I'm interested in the process by which we assign meaning to objects and events," Warren said. "I usually combine multiple images in an attempt to reflect that complexity of experience. This combining can create new and sometimes unexpected meanings."

Lately Warren has focused his work on shadows. "I like the way they describe the object that creates them along with the surface of the object on which they are cast."

Recent Career Highlights:

- 2005: 33rd Annual National Juried Photographic Exhibit, Larson Gallery, Yakima, Washington
- 2005: Kittitas County Annual Juried Exhibit, Gallery One Visual Arts Center, Ellensburg, Washington
- 1995 to present: Richard Warren Graphic Services, owner, Ellensburg, Washington

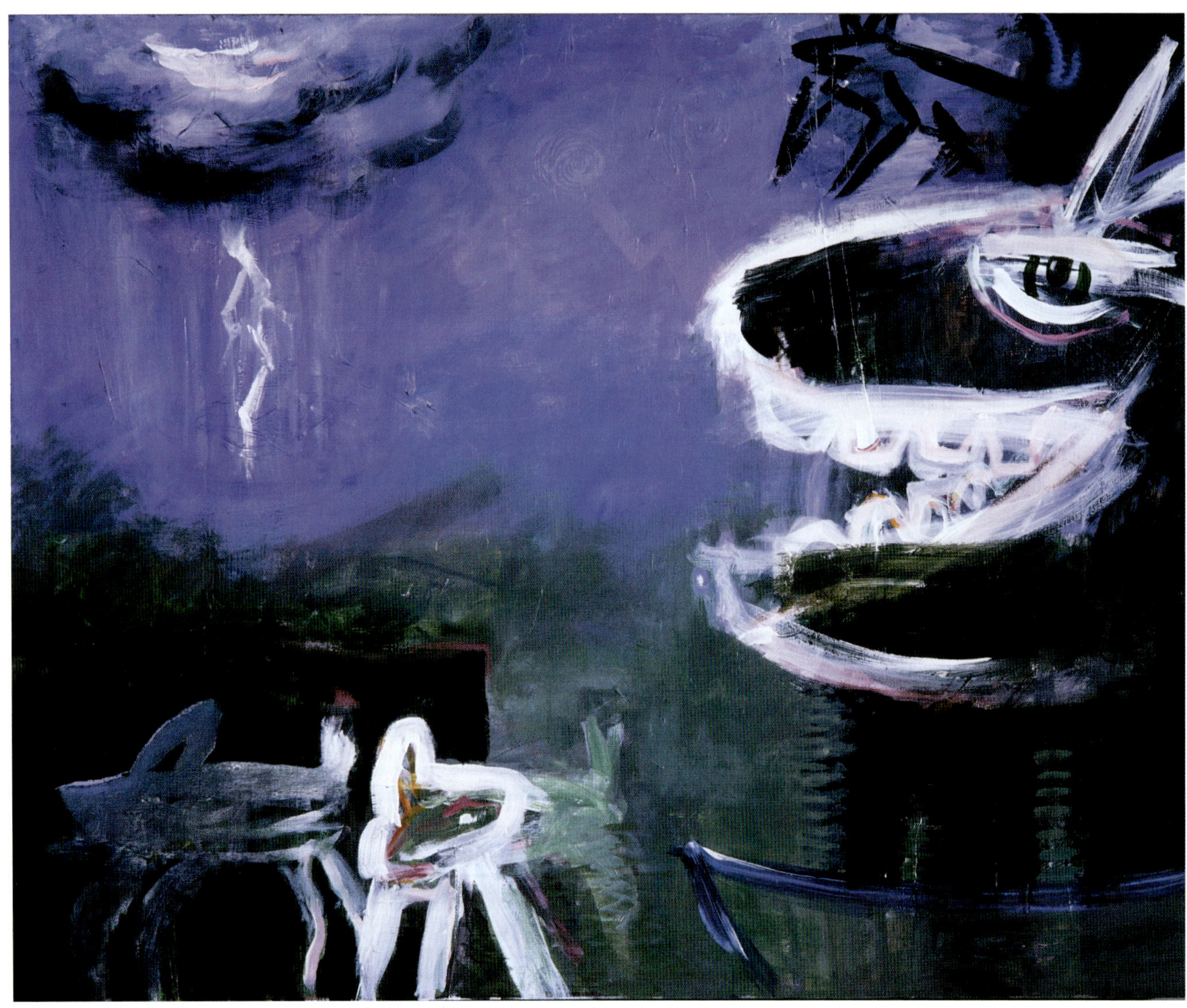

Deluge, 2006, mixed media on masonite, 41 x 33 in.

Ron Westman
Class of 1979

Ocean City, Washington resident Ron Westman spent his life in rural Washington State, which has influenced his work as a painter over the years.

“I have had a lifelong and passionate connection to the non-human aspect of nature. I often use animal forms as symbols in an attempt to address underlying, perhaps primal, human impulses, since, I believe, at particular social levels, we have much in common with other animals.”

His paintings have been on display in several solo and group exhibitions, and are in many private collections, primarily in California and New York. His work has also been acquired by corporate and civic collections, including Microsoft, in Seattle, Washington, and the City of San Francisco Hall of Justice, Robin Bradford Associates, PLM Corporation, and Herb Bradshaw Associates, all located in San Francisco, California.

“I paint mostly in oils, recently acrylics, which I have modified with traditional mediums. I apply these materials with brushes and palette knives to canvas, plywood, or Masonite. Ordinarily, I do not have a specific image or idea in mind. As an expressionist, I work gesturally or intuitively,” Westman said.

Recent Career Highlights:

- 2007: Vermont Studio Center one-month artist retreat, Johnson, Vermont
- 2006: Artwork at MP Marshall Gallery, Aberdeen, Washington
- 2004: Artwork at Salon Maude, Ocean Shores, Washington

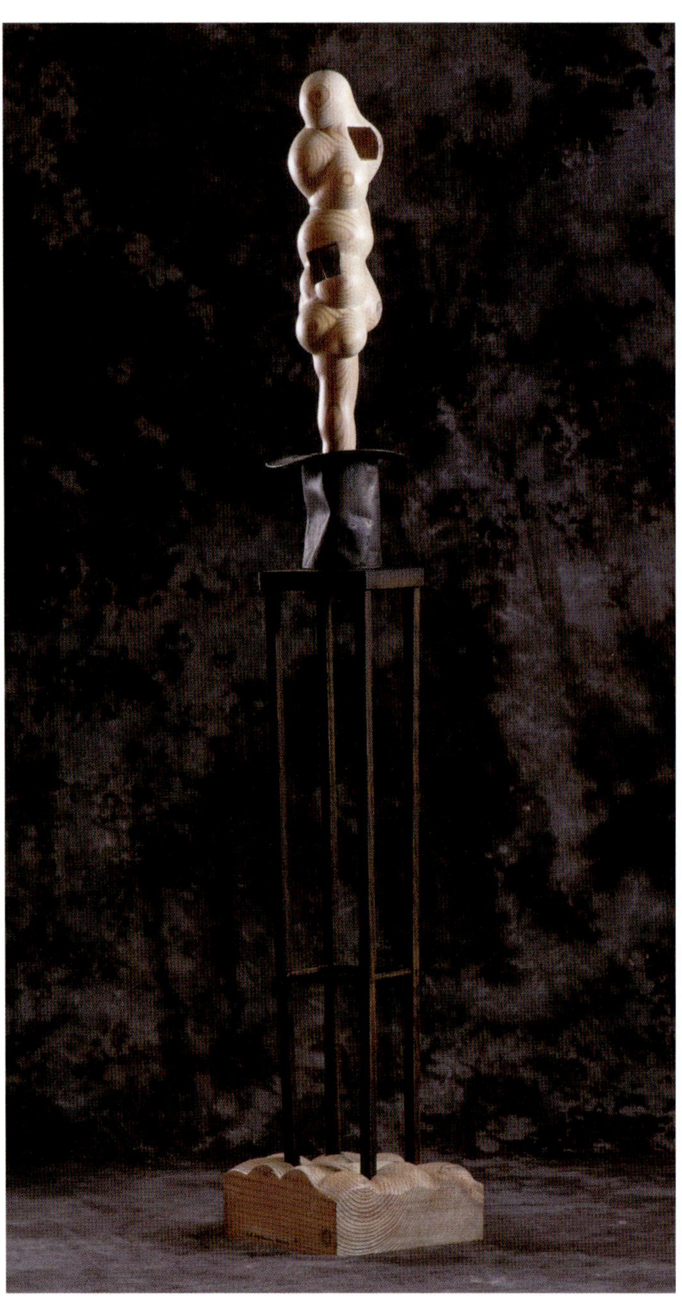

Fog, 2005, carved wood and altered copper toilet float,
11¾ x 11¾ x 70¾ in.

Edward Wicklander

Class of 1975 and 1978

Edward Wicklander's whimsical, multi-media artwork is found throughout the Pacific Northwest, and makes regular appearances at Seattle, Washington's Greg Kucera Gallery, where he has had numerous solo exhibits.

Most of his pieces, primarily sculptures, tell stories—some obvious, some subtle. He often takes literal ideas and places them into strange, unreal situations, forcing the viewer to see the objects in a new light.

"This work reflects themes I keep returning to in my sculpture: the metaphorical value implicit in the materials themselves and my concerns with a loss of human identity in an ever-complex and faster-moving society," Wicklander said.

The Seattle resident primarily works with ceramics, copper and other metals, fiberglass, plastic, glass, plaster, wood, and rubber. His pieces are in several collections, including Microsoft in Redmond, Washington, the Seattle Arts Commission, Swedish Hospital in Seattle, the Valley National Bank in Phoenix, Arizona, the Washington State Arts Commission in Olympia, Washington, and the Frederick R. Weisman Foundation of Art in Los Angeles, California.

Recent Career Highlights:

- 1993-1997: Sculptor instructor, Cornish College of the Arts, Seattle, Washington
- 1993: Artist Trust Gap Grant, Seattle, Washington
- 1988: National Endowment for the Arts Individual Artist's Fellowship Grant in Sculpture

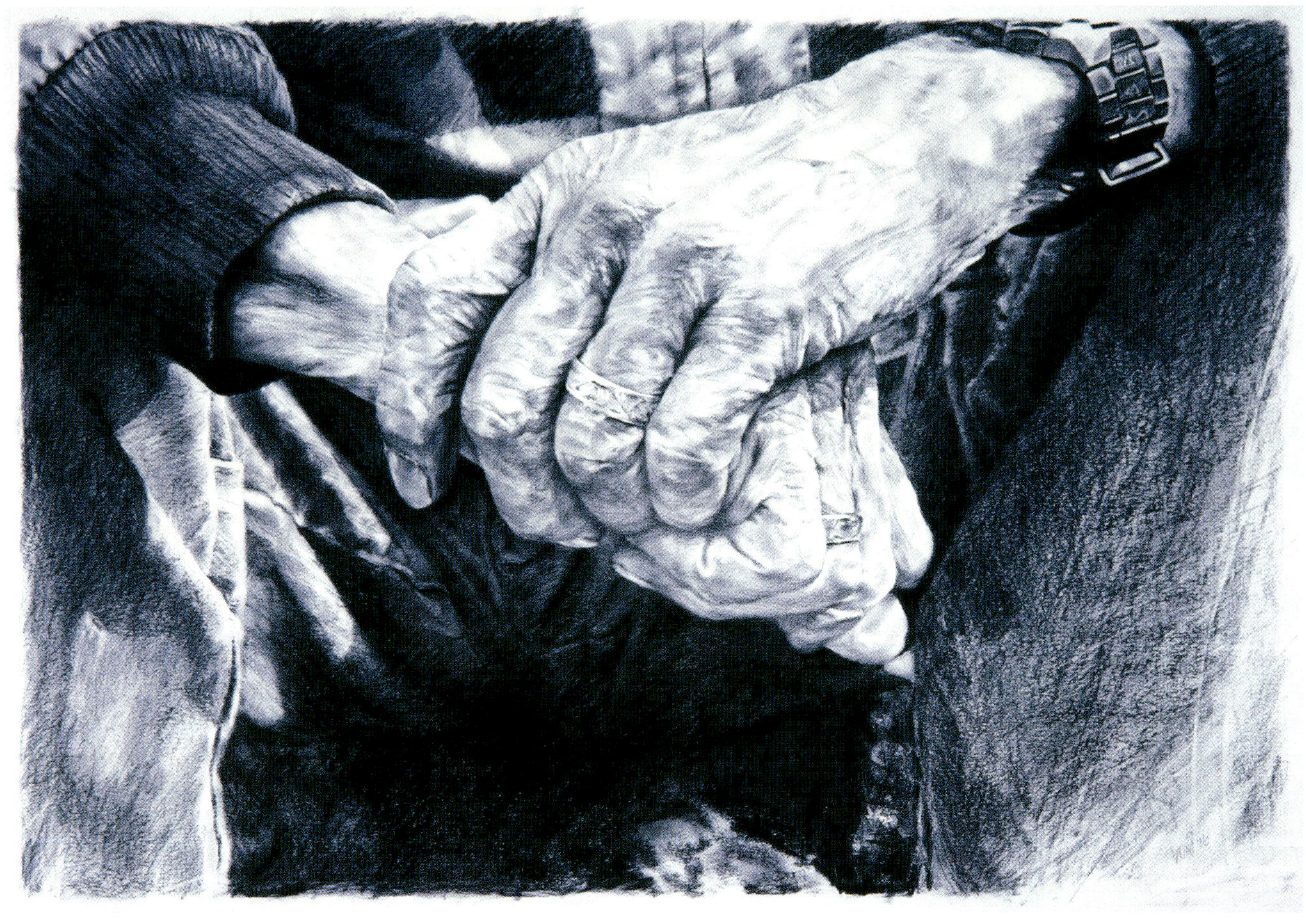

Alvin's Hands, 2006, graphite on paper, 36½ x 24½ in.

Carol Wild-DeLano

Class of 1976 and 1979

Carol Wild-DeLano has spent most of her professional career teaching fine arts and graphic design at Columbia High School in White Salmon, Washington, as well as drawing, painting, and sculpture at Columbia Gorge Community College in The Dalles, Oregon.

"While I plan to continue teaching at least part time at the college level, I look forward to having more time to focus on my work in graphite and paint mediums, and to begin several large projects in graphite documenting Yakama, Klickitat, Wasco, and Chinook Native American women working in the traditional female arts. I also plan to work with Native American fishermen on the Columbia and Klickitat rivers as part of another series," she said.

For the past twenty years, she has taught full time, raised two sons, and worked primarily on commissions. She moved to the Columbia Gorge from Seattle in 1980 to teach, and still loves the area, she said.

"While I have loved being an educator, I am also excited to embark on this next leg of my journey—retirement from public education."

Wild-DeLano earned a master of fine arts degree in drawing and printmaking, as well as a bachelor's degree in fine arts from Central Washington University. In 1978, she taught at Central as an adjunct professor.

Recent Career Highlights:

- 2006: Solo exhibit, West Wind Gallery, The Dalles, Oregon
- 2005: Solo exhibit, Sprint/Baker Gallery, White Salmon, Washington
- 1987: Brooklyn Museum of Modern Art invitational, Works in Graphite exhibition, Brooklyn, New York

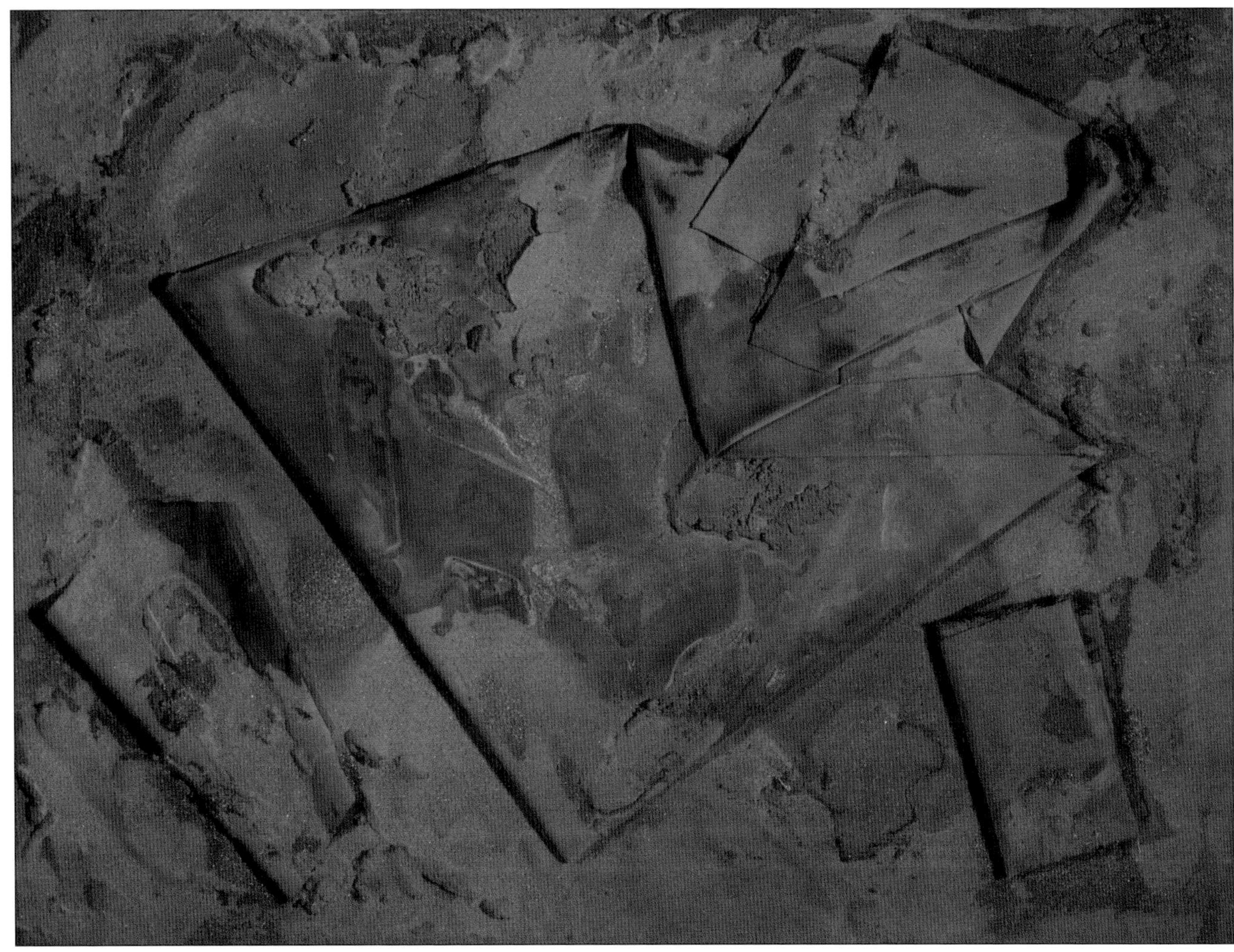

Untitled, 2000, fabric, copper, and ash on wood, 32 x 23½ in.

Ted Wiprud

Class of 1962

Ted Wiprud, a Corvallis, Oregon artist, has spent ten years "using primary colors mixed with natural copper for paintings, and copper mixed with volcanic ash for sculptures."

"My art also consists of photographs of my sculptures, which are made to stand alone as individual pieces. My goal is to make my art contemplative and, on some level, beautiful," he said.

After obtaining a master of fine arts degree in 1964 at Claremont Graduate School in Claremont, California, Wiprud went on to exhibit in many locations, such as Marylhurst College in Marylhurst, Oregon, and at the Northwest Summer Festival at the Seattle Art Museum in Seattle, Washington. His artwork can also be found in several public collections, including Oregon State University in Corvallis, Oregon, the Woodland Park Zoo in Seattle, the Larson Gallery in Yakima, Washington, and at Hewlett-Packard in Corvallis, Oregon.

Recent Career Highlights:

- 2006: Oregon State University Art Emeriti Exhibition, Fairbanks Gallery, Corvallis, Oregon
- 2004: Taking Shape: Contemporary Sculptors, Benton County Museum, Philomath, Oregon
- 2002: Ted Wiprud, Retrospective, Fairbanks Gallery, Corvallis, Oregon

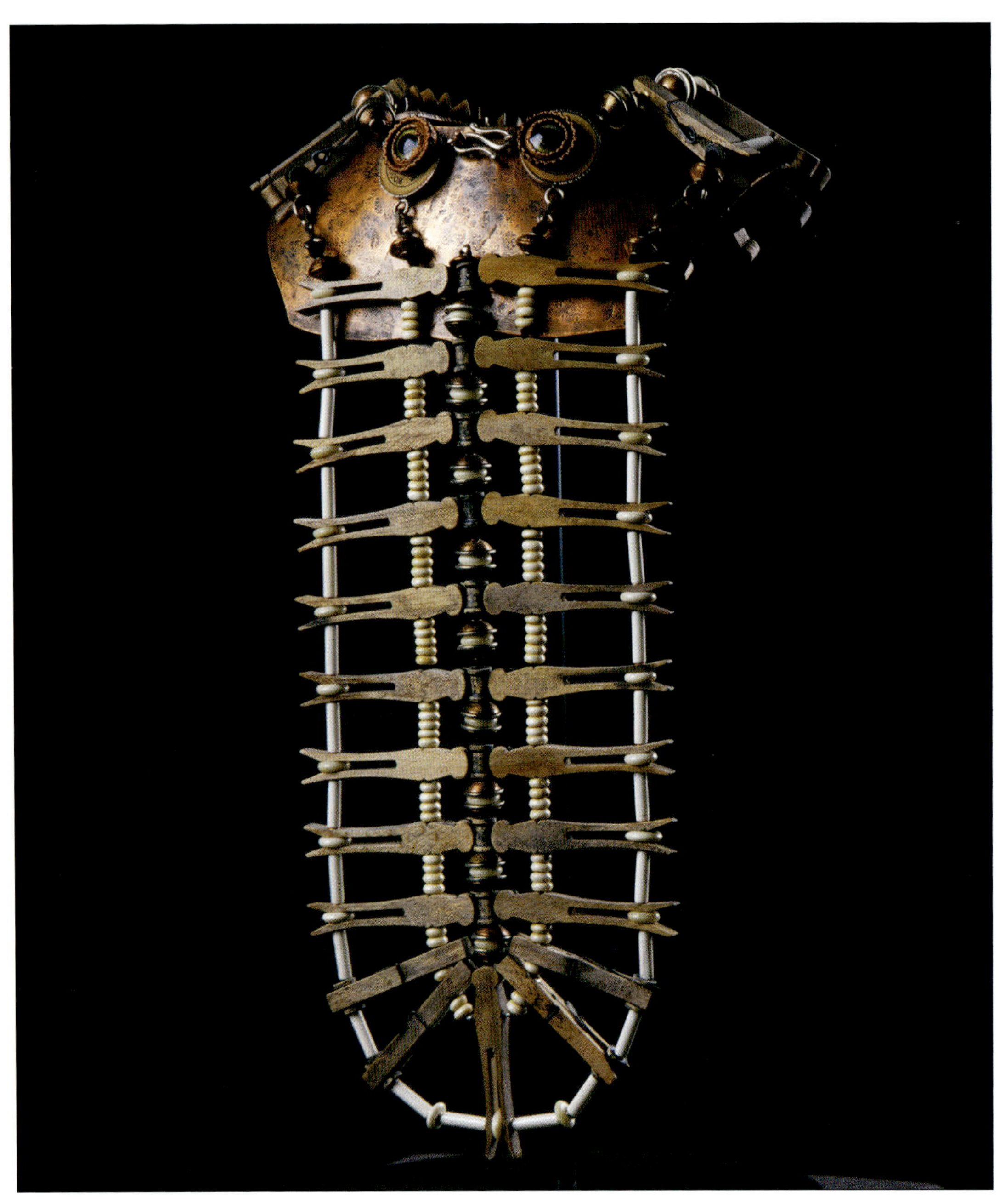

Exosquellette #2, 2003, silver, copper, bone, wood, glass, and nickel, $10\frac{3}{4}$ x 12 x 1 in.

Nancy Worden

Class of 1977

Internationally recognized jewelry artist Nancy Worden said several major themes have crept into the last thirty years of her work, including visual metaphors, personal narratives, references to historical jewelry, and movement.

"I often incorporate found objects from contemporary culture to provide the work with a specific time and place, as well as a vehicle for color," Worden said. "My artwork is a response to the specific events in my life. For these, I try to distill the essence of my experience into something universal to all human experience, or at least the American females of my generation."

Worden, who lives in Seattle, Washington, has shown her work in numerous solo and group exhibitions. She has also been featured in multiple publications, with a recent 2006 feature article in *Metalsmith* magazine.

Worden also won an Artist Trust Fellowship in 2005, and in 2004 she was named Distinguished Alumni Award Winner for the College of Arts and Humanities at Central Washington University.

Recent Career Highlights:

- 2006: Group exhibition, Challenging the Chatelaine, Design Museo, Helsinki, Finland
- 2006: Group exhibition, The Necklace Show, Velvet da Vinci, San Francisco, California
- 2005: Solo exhibition, Modern Artifacts, William Traver Gallery, Seattle, Washington

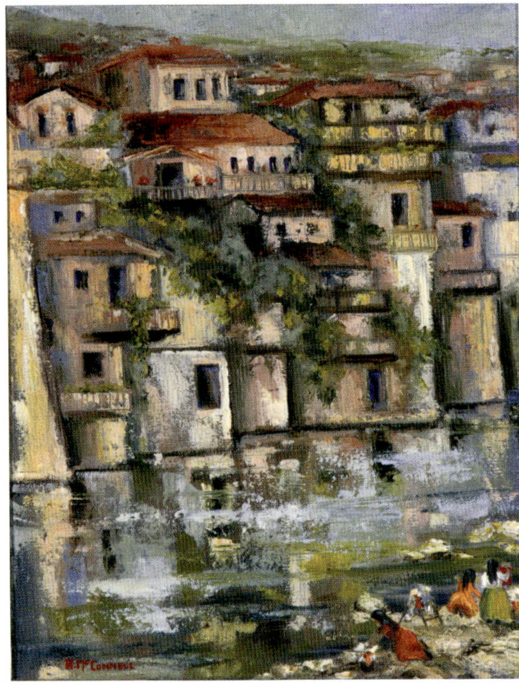

Alma McConnell
Puerto Vallarta, n.d., oil on canvas, 15½ x 19½ in.

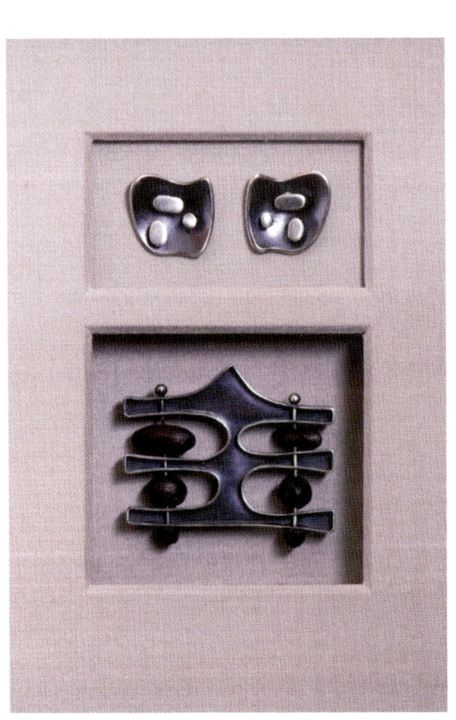

Reino Randall
Pin and Earrings, Central Washington University permanent collection, ca. 1950, silver with wooden beads

Sarah Spurgeon
Six Navels, 1968, mixed media, 9 x 50½ x 2¾ in.

Alma McConnell

1905-2006

Born in Charleston, West Virginia, Alma McConnell earned a master's degree in art from Central Washington University and was the wife of Dr. Robert E. McConnell, President of CWU from 1931 to 1959.

McConnell grew up studying art at an early age yet decided later in life to pursue an education degree. Eventually she returned to the art world, and in 1959, after earning her master's degree, joined the faculty of San Francisco State University. While there, she experimented with clay and wood sculpture, mosaic, cast jewelry, watercolor and oil painting, batik, and collage.

Reino Randall

1911-1997

In 1929 Reino Randall began studying at Central Washington University and graduated from the College of Education in 1934. After teaching art for two years at Wapato Junior High School in Wapato, Washington, he returned to Ellensburg in 1938. That fall, he joined the faculty at Central and remained until his retirement in 1976.

Active in promoting the arts, Randall served on several boards, including the National Art Education Association.

To honor Randall's contributions to the art program at Central, the Board of Trustees named the art building Randall Hall.

Sarah Spurgeon

1903-1985

Sarah Spurgeon was a professor of painting, drawing, and art education in the Department of Art at Central Washington University between 1939 and 1971.

She was honored as professor emeritus upon her retirement in 1971, and in 1977, CWU paid further tribute to her contributions by creating the Sarah Spurgeon Gallery in Randall Hall.

Her artwork is in many private collections and remains on display on the CWU campus. The Ellensburg arts community continues to remember Spurgeon's steady devotion to her students and commitment to their work and careers in art.

INDEX

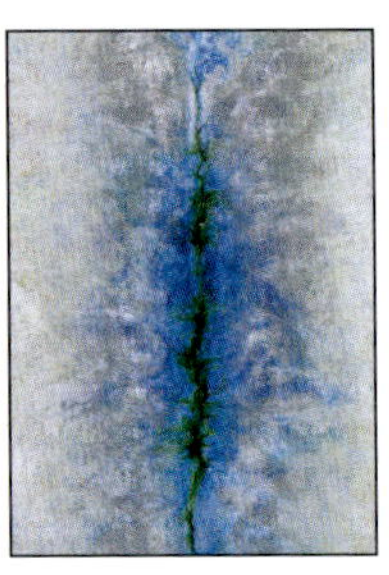
p.p.: 8-9, Albright

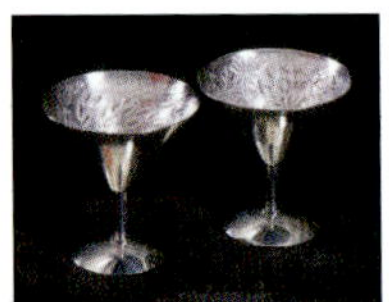
p.p.: 10-11, Beardslee

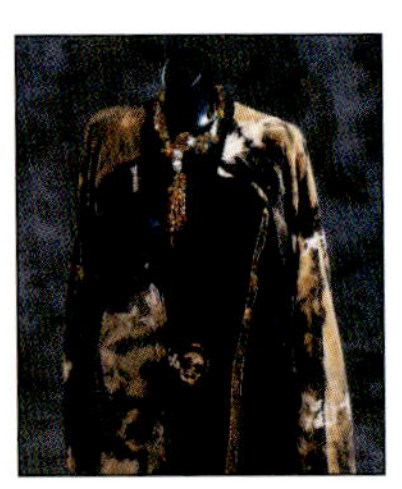
p.p.: 12-13, Bowker

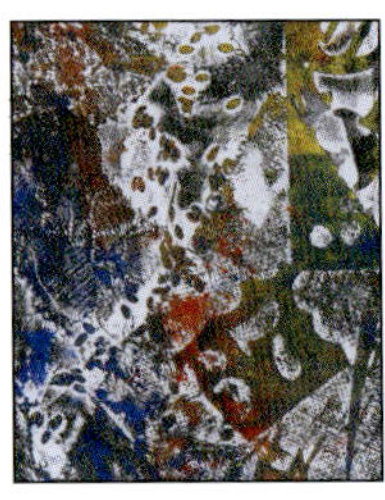
p.p.: 14-15, Bravetti

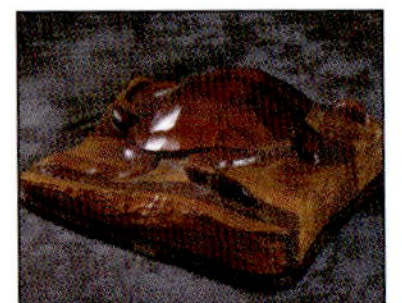
p.p.: 16-17, Brodin

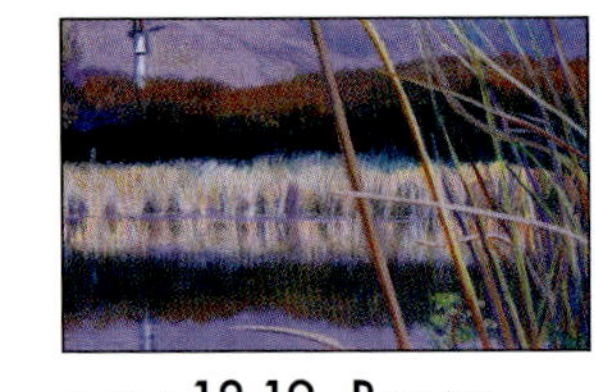
p.p.: 18-19, Brown

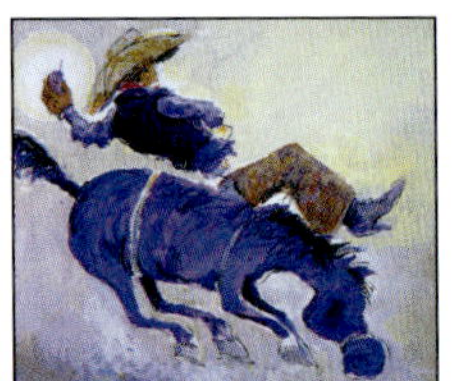
p.p.: 20-21, Campbell

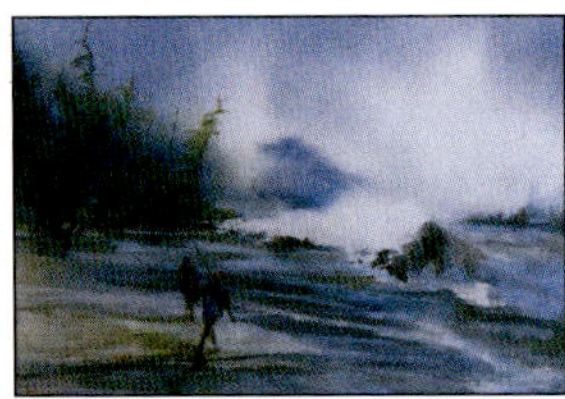
p.p.: 22-23, Christen

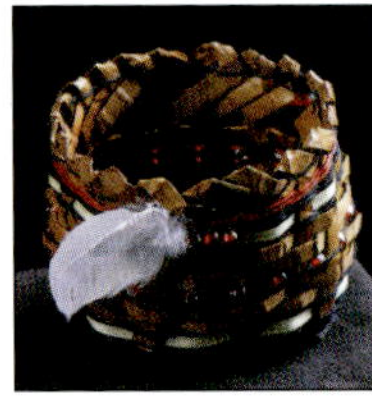
p.p.: 24-25, Cross

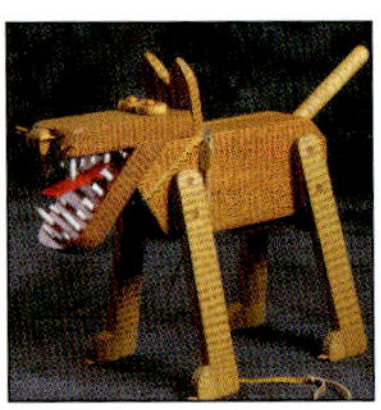
p.p.: 26-27, Davis

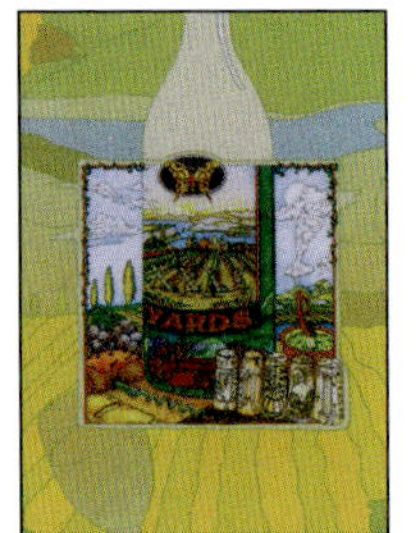
p.p.: 28-29, Dietrich

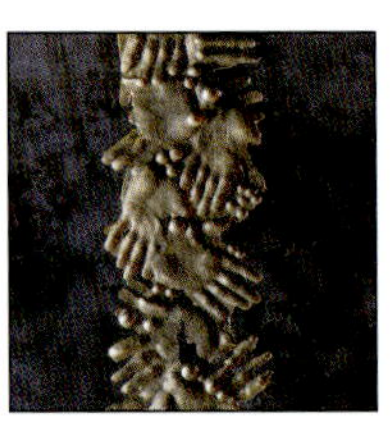
p.p.: 30-31, Dilley

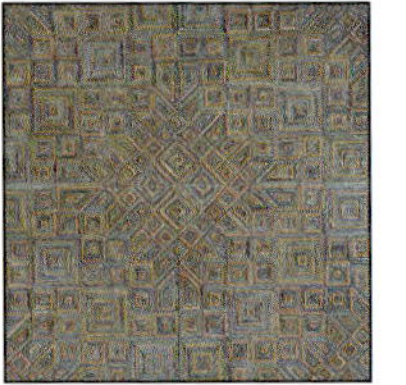
p.p.: 32-33, Elliott

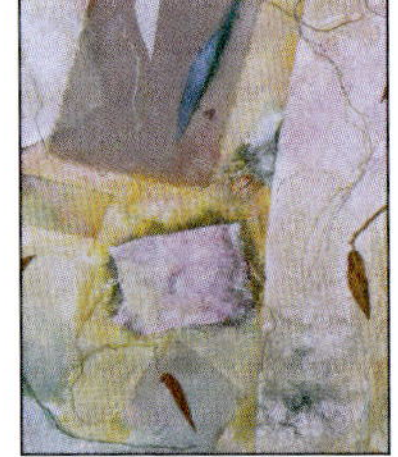
p.p.: 34-35, Foster

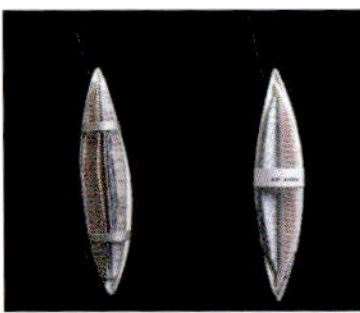
p.p.: 36-37, Goodboy

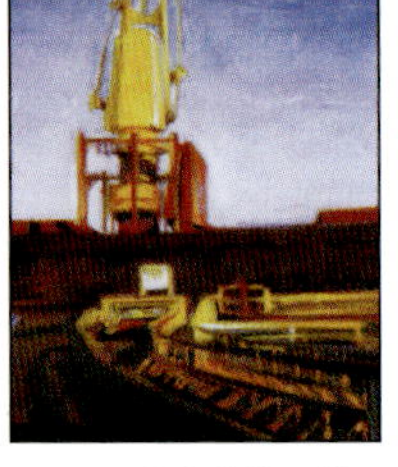
p.p.: 38-39, Grebmeier

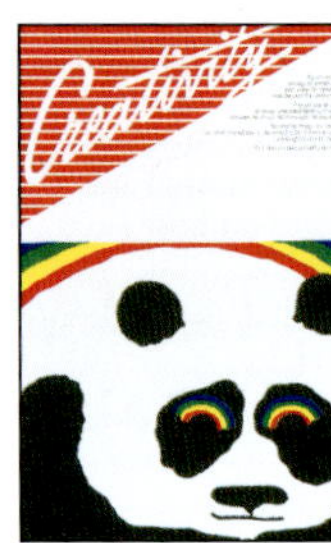

p.p.: 40-41, Henson

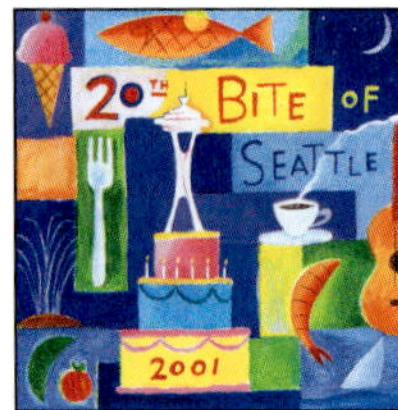

p.p.: 42-43, Hinrichs

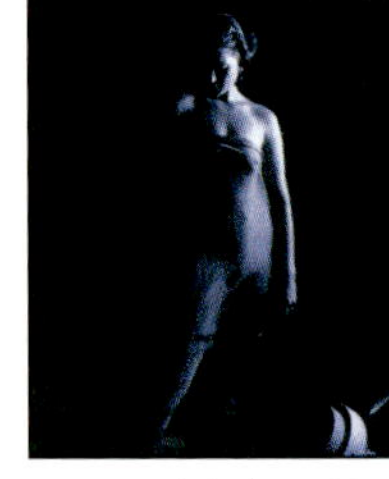
p.p.: 44-45, Hodge

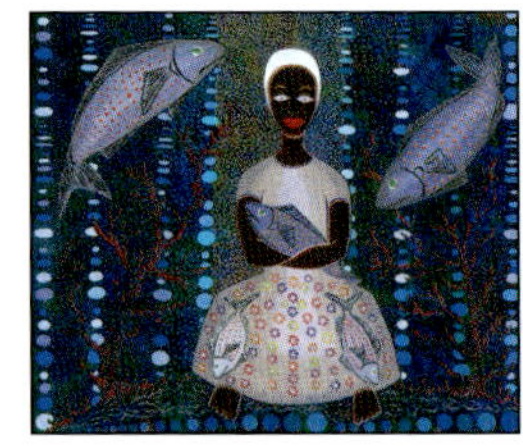
p.p.: 46-47, Johnson

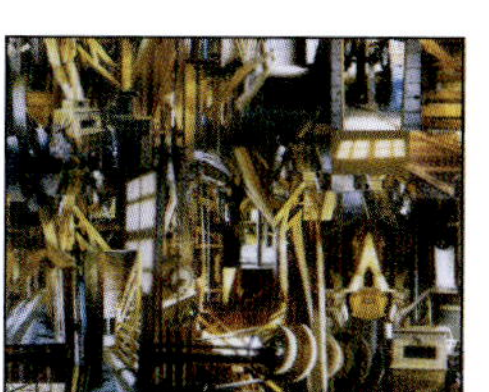
p.p.: 48-49, Johnson

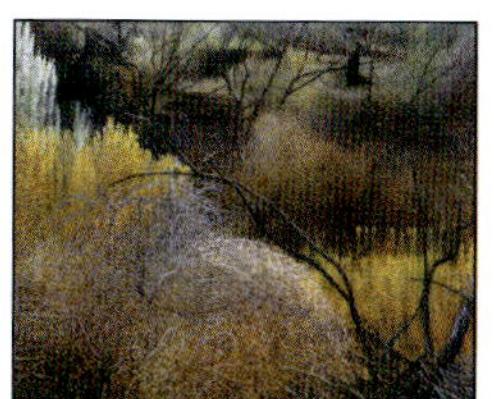
p.p.: 50-51, Jones

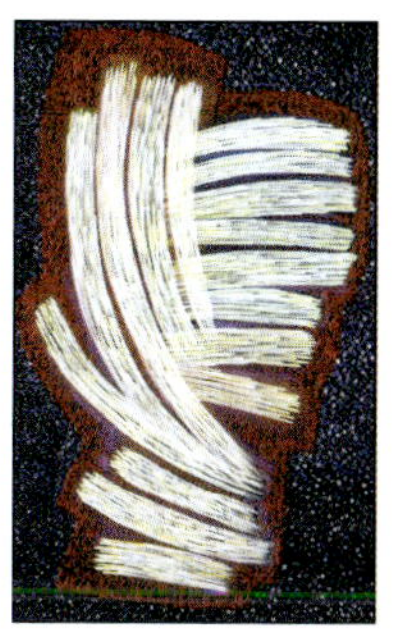
p.p.: 52-53, LaMar

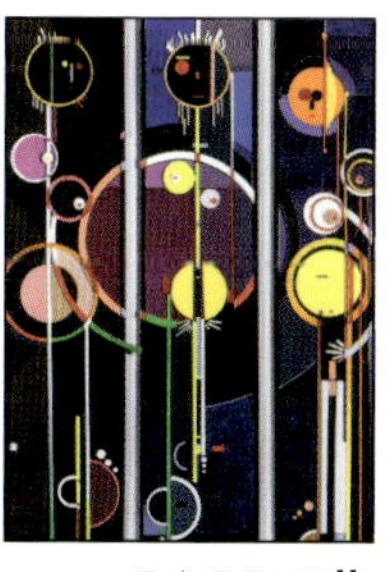
p.p.: 54-55, Lilley

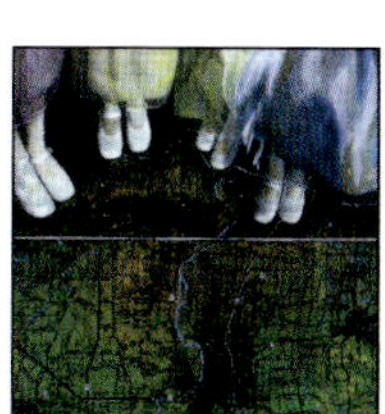
p.p.: 56-57, Loomis Dietz

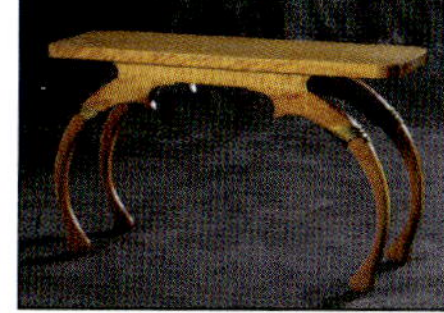
p.p.: 58-59, Louise

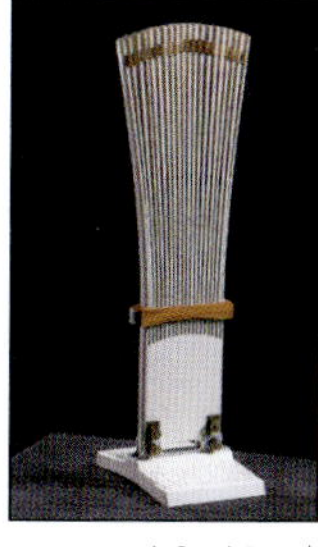
p.p.: 60-61, Maakestad

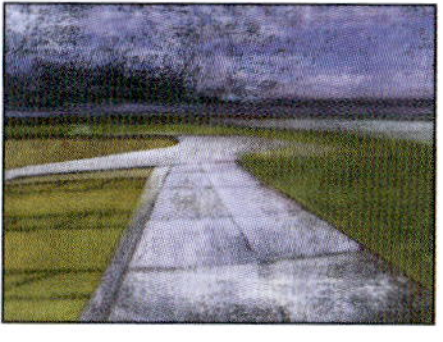
p.p.: 62-63, Maakestad

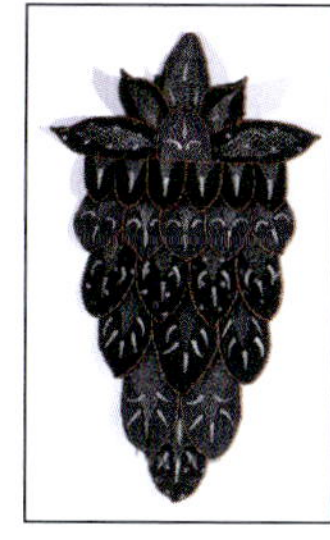
p.p.: 64-65, MacKenzie

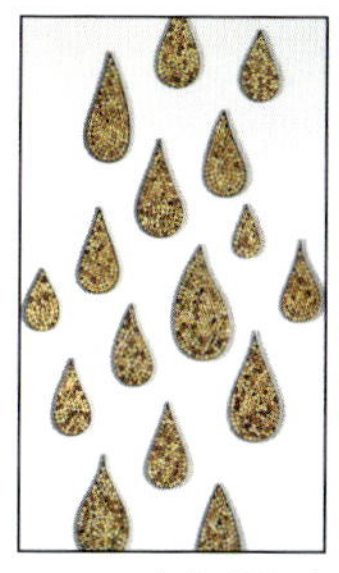
p.p.: 66-67, McCall

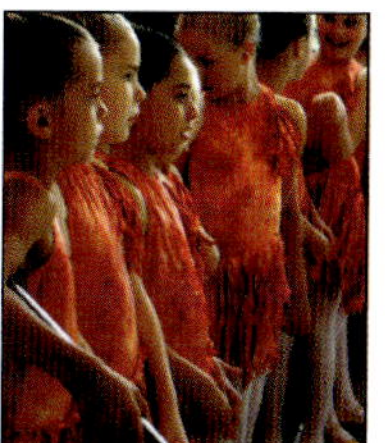
p.p.: 68-69, McTimmons

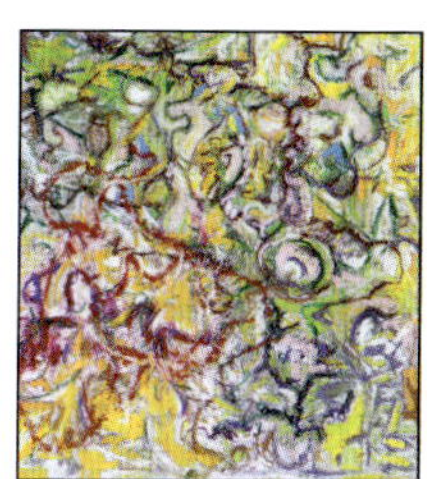
p.p.: 70-71, Meyers

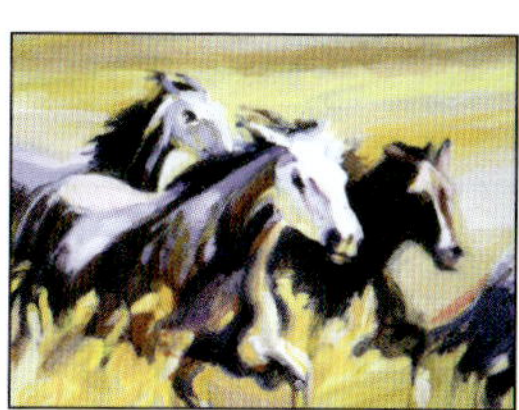
p.p.: 72-73, Meyers

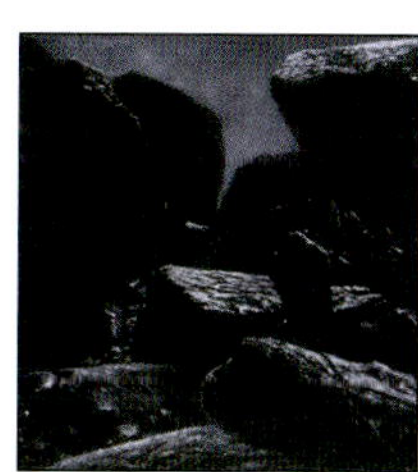
p.p.: 74-75, Moen

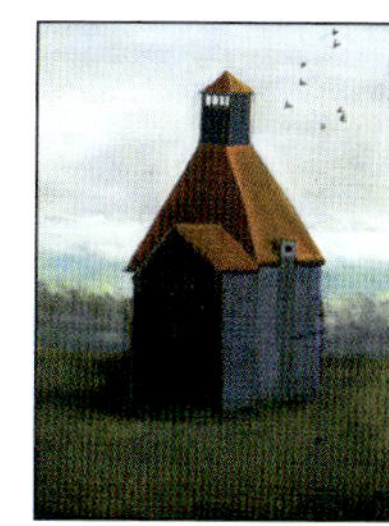
p.p.: 76-77, Morgan

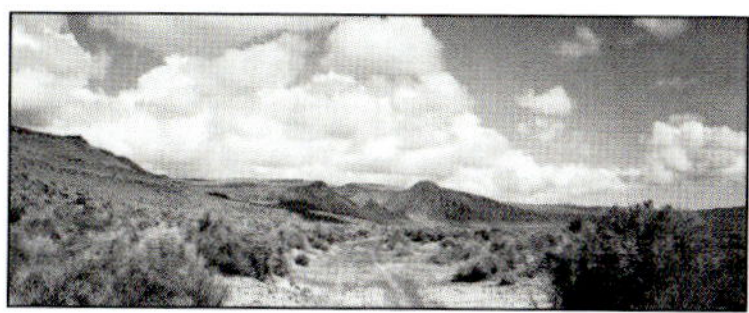
p.p.: 78-79, Norlin

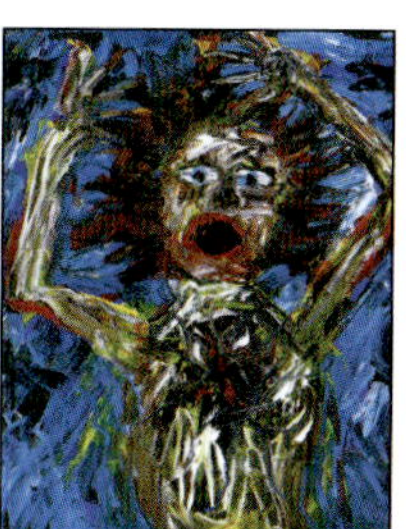
p.p.: 80-81, Orleman

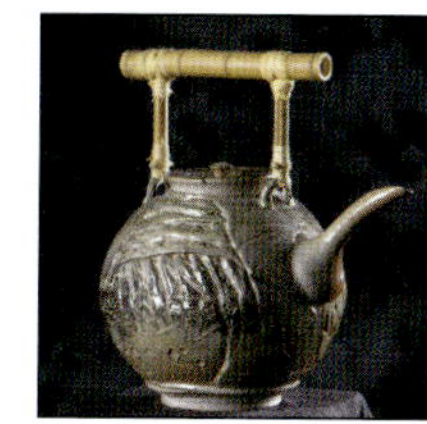
p.p.: 82-83, Osier

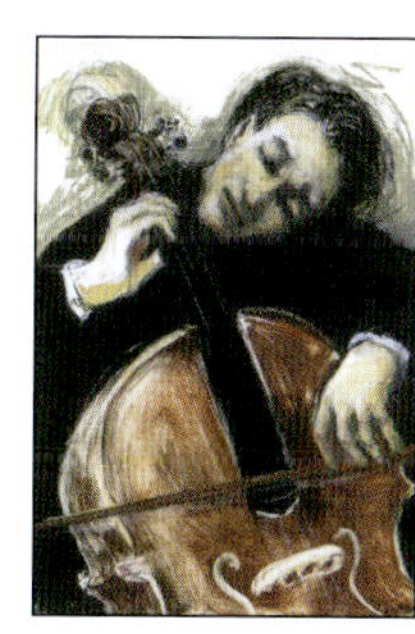
p.p.: 84-85, Otto

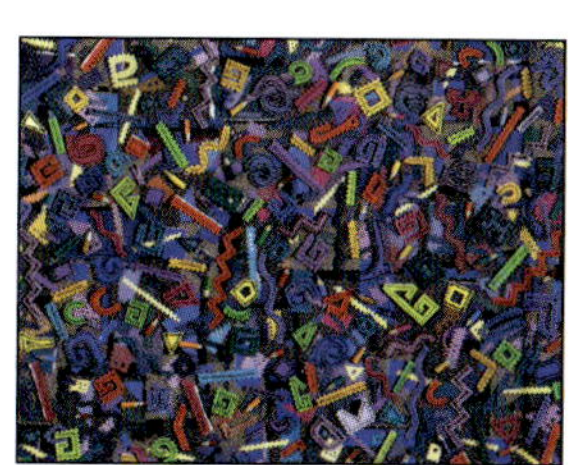
p.p.: 86-87, Purser

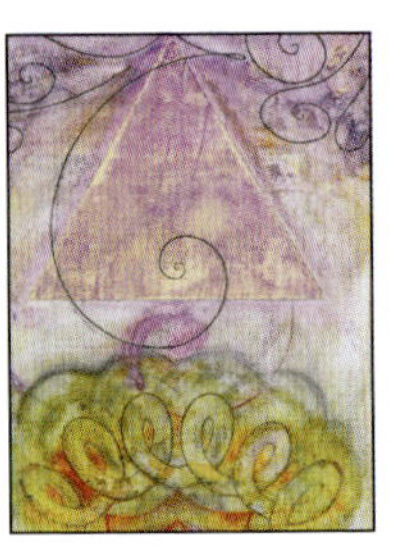
p.p.: 88-89, Ritchie

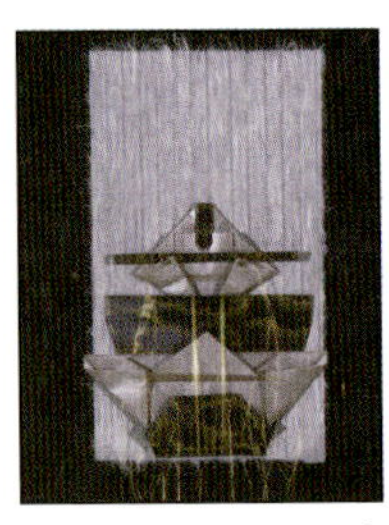
p.p.: 90-91, Schaake

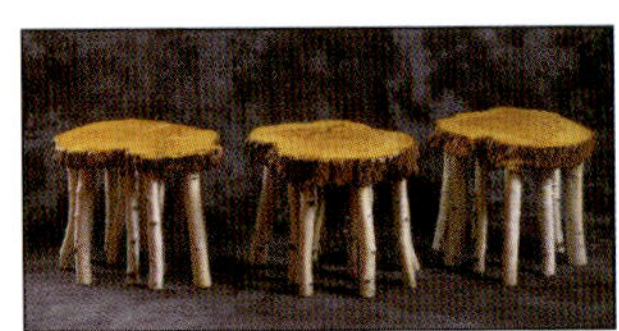
p.p.: 92-93, Shambacher

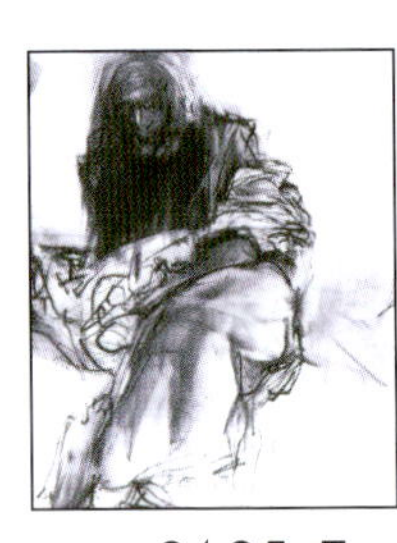
p.p.: 94-95, Tempero Schmidt

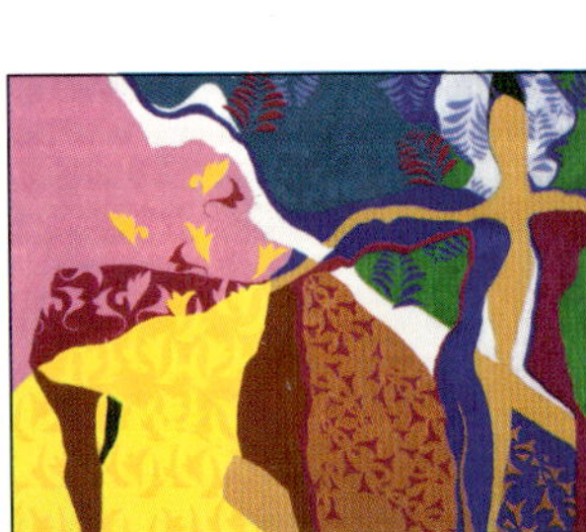
p.p.: 96-97, Singleton

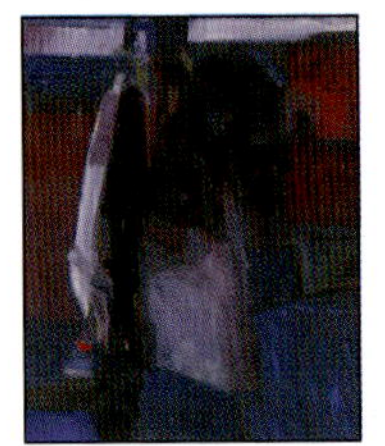
p.p.: 98-99, Smith

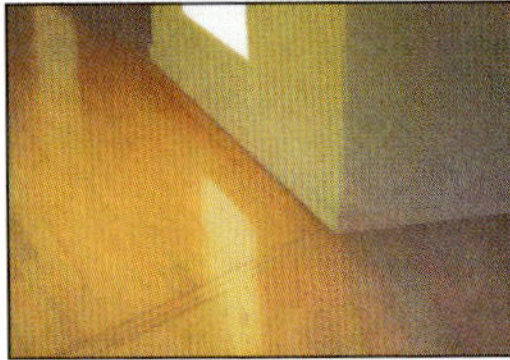
p.p.: 100-101, Speth

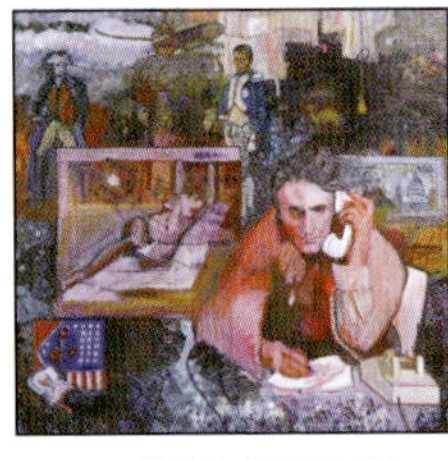
p.p.: 102-103, Tayer

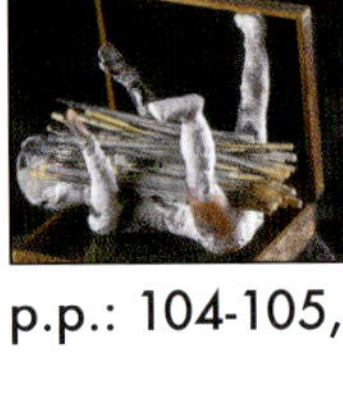
p.p.: 104-105, Timo

p.p.: 106-107, Tompkins

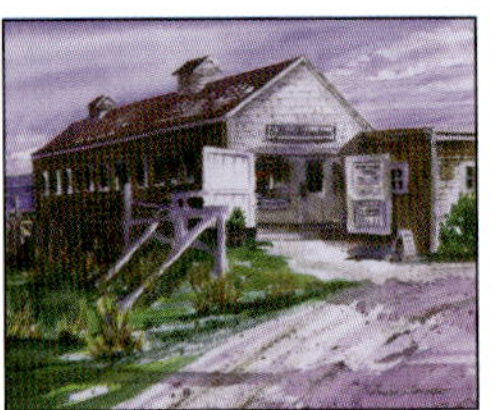
p.p.: 108-109, Tornow

p.p.: 110-111, Rock-Waddington

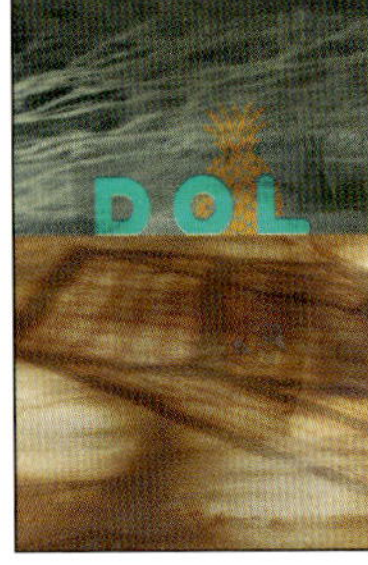

p.p.: 112-113, Warren

p.p.: 114-115, Westman

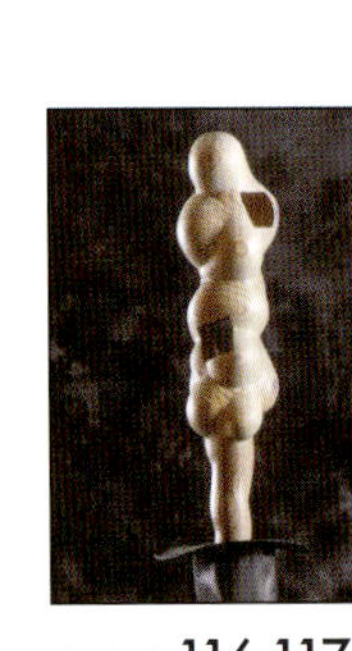
p.p.: 116-117, Wicklander

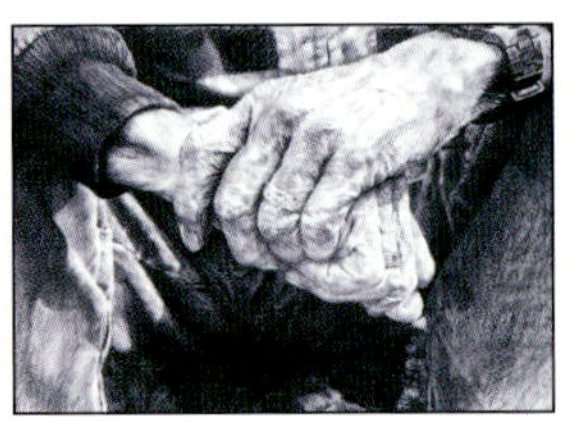
p.p.: 118-119, Wild-DeLano

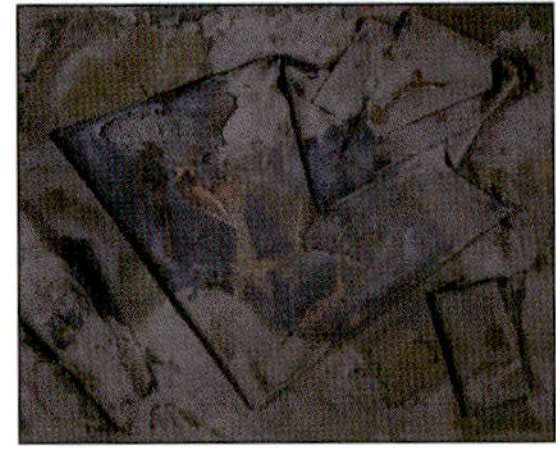
p.p.: 120-121, Wiprud

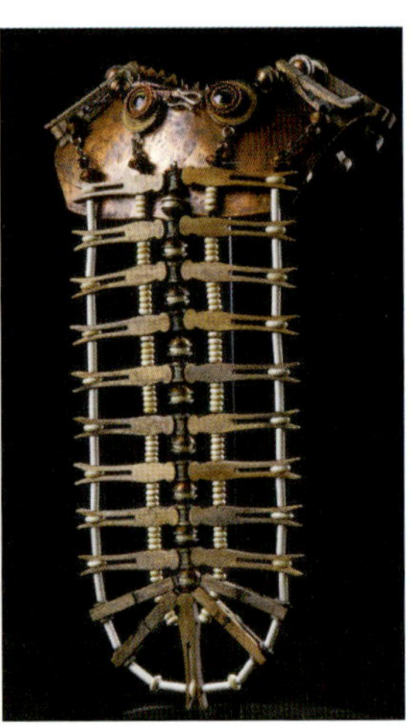
p.p.: 122-123, Worden

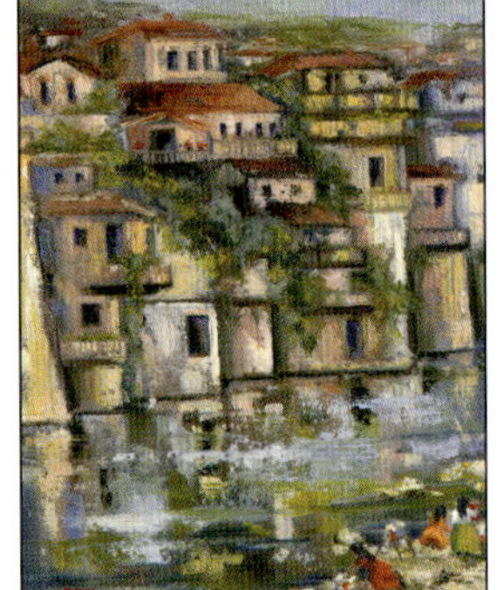
p.p.: 126, McConnell

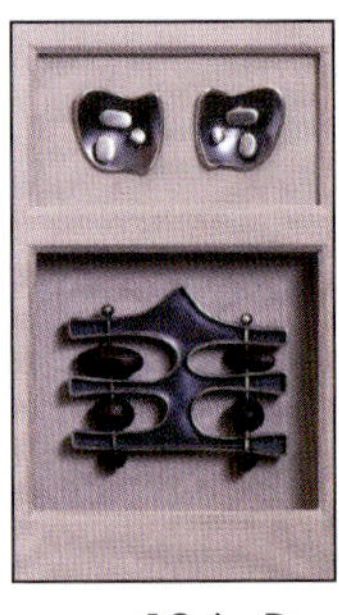
p.p.: 126, Randall

p.p.: 126, Spurgeon